Kaleidoscope:

Mirroring Fragments

Poems New & Revisioned

Walt Bado

Lexington, Kentucky

Dedicated
To My Spiritual
Companions On The Way

To family members, all so dear;
And friends, acquaintances, far and near;
To spiritual companions on the way,
An opening word for eye and ear.

We dwell on Earth a passing day--
With shining sun, if blessed, "make hay";
And at the end arrives good Night,
When we must leave our house of clay.

May she come--not to affright--
With hope of heavenly delight.
May she come, Love's final call
To ready selves for morning light.

Foreword

In a time of division on many fronts, and in the lurking shadows of M.A.D. with its potential atomization of the world, I present this select collection of my poems in a spirit of hope.

People, places, things, and events of all sorts have left their mark on me, now in my early nineties. Recalled on the following pages, they are in retrospect (and prospect) bits and pieces of my life--my microcosmic, personal kaleidoscope introduced in the opening double poem.

The universe of which we human beings are infinitesimal parts is itself--such is my hopeful vision throughout--a cosmic kaleidoscope: a whole, the multitudinous bits and pieces of which are kin to one another, reflect one another, each simultaneously contributing to the unity and beauty of the whole. As the subtitle further denotes: the universe involves an ongoing dynamic process of growth and integration: its coming-to-be is suffused with the light of the immanent-transcendent cosmic Energy called by many a name, beyond all naming.

Full disclosure: I am a native Chicagoan, of Slovakian immigrant stock, a Jesuit priest retired from the philosophy classroom (Xavier University, Cincinnati, Ohio) and campus ministry (University of Kentucky, Lexington). Until recently, I was engaged in full-time spiritual direction in the Catholic Diocese of Lexington.

For over seventy years, I have complemented my intellectual pursuits with the reading and composing of poems as both avocation and source of recreation. One result has been a growing collection of poems, some of which have been published; others arranged for private distribution. This book is presented to a wider audience, including my spiritual directees, companions on the way; to them the book is dedicated.

TABLE OF CONTENTS

A

Things and People of All Sorts

B

Matters of All Sorts that Matter

C

All Manner of Things That Matter Will Be Well

Things and People of All Sorts

Opening Perspectives on Being a Fragment

My Lawn Mower and Me

materialist
or pantheist
i'm not--i'm only
      limited me
male caucasian
in the u-s-of-a nation
      under God a human subject
      by God nobody's object
and yet--alas for me--
in summer gardening's spree
      i want to mow the lawn
      right after dawn
but that mower of mine objects
to whatever yours truly projects

A Platonist Going to the Dogs

I love to contemplate
Eternal Forms of Plato
Singly and as a Whole,
The after-burners of my Soul
Switched on especially
By Goodness/Beauty.

But more and more I see
The (Neo)Platonist in me
Becoming Rover and Fido
Riding in the family auto,
Agog at passing things--keen
On the changing scene.

My Fishing Tree

Beside the cloistered pond I'm blessed to fish,
An oak keeps company. Squirrels scurry along
Its branches, blackbirds with crimson epaulets
Make calls, bobwhite in fields nearby take note.

Weathered and old, this our common host,
A lightning scar zigzagging down its gnarled
Trunk; at its base lie broken limbs, decaying
Bark, scattered acorn shells, leaves of bygone years.

Amazing tree! Standing its ground in season
After season, welcoming all who visit.
Long have I longed to lose myself in it,
Be one with it, breathe in its spirit.

Now, as another bassing sabbath ends,
The western sun embraces my fishing tree.
Evening shadows close around it. Softly, shyly,
Young stars emerge, dance amid its branches.

Encounter at Dawn in Athens

On a path to the Parthenon
I came upon
a little lizard at play
in the new sun's spray--
suddenly still,
fixed by the fall
of my shadow.

From below
it watched me,
silently,
head held high,
vigilant of eye,
its body tensed,
for me condensed

to the matter of presence.
Is it providence
or chance,
sheer happenstance,
that we encounter
a given other;
and even

more basic given,
that we, and all
we encounter, be at all?
I too had paused,
for a long moment lost
in the question; and then,
pursuing again

my way,
I frightened the question away.

Threnody and Melody

From under Vatican eaves sounds the mourning
Of doves in friar-grey. Francis in Rome,
Inspired by Francis of Assisi, pleads with us,
Fellow earthlings, to look closely around us
And see the evil we are doing to our planet;
And what we singly, and all together, can do
To undo the evil.

With *Sputnik* and *Apollo* we have new eyes.
We have begun to see, from out in space,
The beauty of our earthly home--a cosmic
Ornament, luminescent in the darkness.
Like little children, awed by their first Christmas
Tree fully ablaze, we have cause to celebrate.
Earth so beautiful.

And destructible. Oil spills, forests afire,
Melting mountains, plastic-glutted oceans,
And Lazarus lying outside Dives' mansion,
Dying in rotting rags. Threnody of destruction,
Desecration, of the kaleidoscope of creation
With its known orders--mineral, vegetable,
Animal, human--

Inter-related fragments of a universal
Whole, much of which is still to be known.
In contrast to proverbial Cassandra,
And her chorus of woe, Francis in his twin
Incarnation calls all people of good will
To care for one another; to share Earth's goods
For the good of all;

To dare affirm matter sacred in all
Its dimensions, the mystery of God's
Free and loving self-giving, of God's self-
Emptying, in the divine acts of creation
And redemption--sacred enough to be
Sung in melodious canticle, *Laudato Si'*:
Praise be to you, God.

Before the Fall and After

We have God's word for it. When all was fresh
And green in Eden, God breathed on dust
And Adam came to be, graced with mobility
Of leg and tongue. He could both walk with God
And talk with God in that primeval garden.

Adam could also give animals their names,
Not as tokens of dominion but as ways
To recognize companions at work and play.
At heart, though, He-Man/Adam longed
For a companion, like him, yet unlike him--

A new form of Who-Man to satisfy his holy
Sense of He-Man needs in Eden, paradise
On earth. And then, she came: She-Man Eve.
To whom he now could cleave with all
The longing in him, fulfilled by a new sense

Of belonging to one just like him, but ah,
So different. In view of what happened next,
Was it really she who felled him? Or did the two,
Together, with a conspiring third, really think
They'd ever outwit the One, eat of the forbidden

Tree, and become divine? Pride-full folly!
First of many firsts of raw originality becoming
Rote; Man-and-Woman-Unkind limping
Out of Eden; and for all time damned to suffer
The babble and gabble, the lies and fake news,
All the din and confusion of Babel.

The Cave Art of Lascaux

There are caves, and then there are *caves*,
You betcha--one big one in Kentucky known
As "Mammoth," with stalagmites and stalactites

That stun the eye. But for *art*, there's Lascaux
In southwestern France, with its human creations
From the Paleolithic Era. It was there that I,

On a September day in 1956, lucked out,
Joining two others in a tour with a special guide,
Aunt of one of the boys who, in 1940, chanced upon

The cave complex almost in their own backyards.
Unlocking the entrance, she ushered us in.
And there they were, from thousands of years before.

Now under electric lights, in air-conditioned chamber
After chamber: horses and bison, aurochs and ibex;
Deer, bears, lions, wolves—and mammoths; all

In rich reds, yellows, greens, with black shadings;
Many, tri-dimensional on the contours of the rock
Walls and ceilings. Our good guide expatiating

On the *ur*art and its interpretations, I, amid
The flow of reassuring white noise, found myself
Floating away in reverie, apart yet not alone;

In spirit with, and admiring as I still do,
The creativity and skill of distant kin,
Cro-Magnon Man & Woman come of age.

Considerations

(In Honor of Pierre Teilhard de Chardin)

Haloed by fire, the sun goes down, raising
Eastward on seesaw Earth a wafer-moon.
From thickening night stars emerge, stars
Upon countless stars,

                              extending in boundless
Space. What are these stars? Mindless fires
Or sparks of fires long extinguished, one and all
Indifferent to us, for all our childhood ditties?
Or can fates be spun,

                              and our fortunes told,
By calculating skies? Is it worth our while to try
To trace the signs of cosmic order; and then,
Inspired, to chant a psalm, sing a lover's canticle?
For scientistic reason,

                              honed to be reductive,
Efforts to decode a supposed universal heliogram
Are all too human flights from raw reality;
The universe is a godless void with no
Intrinsic meaning.

                    ****

                              Soft is the night
With mingled garden scents, athrob with crickets,
Warm with the warmth of autumn's lingering sun.
The sun! Star nearest to Earth, our star, centering
Our daily rounds, storied

                              amid the stellar seas
By poets and seers. Eons and eons over, its ardor
Has incandesced in ruby, rose, and fire-coral;
In nautilus, monarch, cardinal, and tiger; in us,
Ourselves, learning

                              to know, yearning to see,
With muted poets and blind seers, a still more
Ancient Fire.

Ionian Pantheon

Sight-seers all, we were prepared to see
The coastal areas of modern Turkey.
But as we tooled along in our tourist bus,
The sites we saw became old Greece for us,

With three-star billing--famed Ionia.
For starters, Izmir, ancient Smyrna,
Birthplace of Homer and his epic stories
Of gods and men at war. And those memories

On memories of Pre-Socratics 101!
Xenophanes and his little Colophon,
Where, learning his religious ABCs,
He smelled out Homer's fishy deities;

Or equally little Clazomenae, equally
Significant, but for incipient cosmology,
Its elementally mindful Anaxagoras
Seeing Mind throughout the universe;

Or Miletus, with Anaximenes proposing Air
As the basic principle found everywhere;
While in reply Anaximander taught
The generating Boundless of his thought;

And Thales floated the idea, Water.
Then, ah! conception-site of that cosmic river
One never enters twice: glorious Ephesus,
Where its great visionary of change, Heraclitus,

Traced eternal Fire and Logos in time's flow;
Where nascent western reason, in its nascent glow,
Was to be enriched by three illustrious Christian
Jews with their faith-inspired vision:

Paul, afire with Christ, crowned his two years spent
In Ephesus with his great love-letter-testament
To the faithful there. John, the Evangelist,
Beloved friend of Jesus, was blessed

In his later years, while in brief exile
In Ephesus, to shelter for the while
The Virgin Mary. Centuries before the Council
Of Ephesus acclaimed it, she, in the still

Depths of her humble and trusting being, stirred
By the Spirit speaking with angelic word,
Affirmed the mystery of matter in time and change,
Mystery of divine and human in awesome exchange:

Co-equal Son of God, eternally divine Logos,
Becoming Man in Woman becoming *Theotokos*.

Tabby in Nazareth

There she was, just inside the entrance
To the basilica commemorating
The traditional site of the first joyful
Mystery—a brindled house cat, purring

As I passed by. Offspring of a long line
Of cats reverting to the household of
The Holy Family? Laugh—but do recall
The joyous wonder that happened there.

Tabby, so much at home in Mary's home,
So welcoming and felicitous a sign!
Sign of the woman hosting a mighty
Angel, her womb becoming home for God.

The Muses and the Trinity

At first, according to Pausanias, three;
Then triple three, springing in Grecian piety
From Father-Zeus and Mnemosyne/Memory:

One and all equally goddesses,
Their synergy suffusing the plethora
Of all our labors in arts and sciences--

Dim intimation of triune mystery
Setting the universe athrob. *Abba*,
Fathering Love in all eternity;

And Son, co-timeless in the Father's glory,
Of Maiden Mary timely born, *Sophia*,
Iconic Wisdom exalted on Calvary;

And co-creative Spirit, Paraclete-Twin,
Inspiring creation's spiral--*Ruah*,
Breathing upon, truing, its easterly spin.

Don Quixote

Still a deluded idealist, tragically comic?
And--to the marketplace's cachinnation--
Still jousting with windmills without grain
In a barren plain without wind?

Realist! With projects down to earth.
The just man and woman justicing,
Intent on confronting at any cost
A protean foe of many disguises.

Knight-errant Quixote today stands up
To Mammon's money-and-power-hungry
Minions, with all their monkey business.
They see only what they want to see,

Hear only what they want to hear, do only
What they want to do, undoing what God
Providently does. Mammon--no longer
Content to steal, in promethean guise,

Fire from heaven. He now ventures far
Into the heavens with world-destructive
Uranium fire-power. Here on planet
Earth, Mammon, continuing his subtle

Masquerade, seduces the all too common
Man and woman co-operating willy-nilly
In his all-consuming enterprises--
At the cost of fauna and flora, forests

And plains; rivers, seas, and once plastic-
Free oceans. Long live Quixote and all
In his company! All who strive to bring
Windmills of all sorts into universal service.

Quixote versus Mammon, no longer riding
Cadaverous Rocinante; but astride the Holy
Spirit, her wings stirring up new, refreshing
Winds, restoring a dying plasticized world
To living, vibrant color.

Mind and Heart in the Universe

Present in the universe, *Mind.* Confirmed
By $E=mc^2$ and scientists' everyday belief
That their research in their chosen fields
Is basically meaningful, even useful.
You just don't undertake something if
You think the enterprise is absurd.

But is there *Heart* at the core of it all?
Of course, it's cute--that polar bear cub,
With those two little round black eyes
And that little black nose in its furry white
Face, as it plays in the snow with its mother.
But even for Victorian Romantics

Nature could be red in tooth and claw.
Nowadays polar ice is melting; polar
Bears--and whales and seals and penguins--
Are threatened by environmental changes.
Across the globe, Mother Earth/Gaia is
Stressing out. But are "tree huggers" only

Dreamy-eyed Romantics gone bonkers?
Is Jane Goodall only a do-goody
Fantasist? Is even Francis of Assisi,
With his *Laudato Si'* and its message
Of grateful love and care for all of God's
Creatures, a sorry specimen of misguided

Humanity? Love, the gift that keeps on giving!
Day in, day out, in all sorts of ways.
No shouting headlines, but heartlines galore.
Those words and deeds--publicly unheard,
Unseen--but quietly, behind the scenes,
Helping our little planet Earth go merrily

Round and round without spinning off into
The void of space. Inklings of a profoundly
Deeper cosmic Word and Deed made human
And historic: *"Love one another as I
Have loved you; there is no greater love . . ."*

Hailing the Waters of the Sunshine State

Water! Ancient sister of Earth, Air, and Fire;
Elemental element and wellspring
From whose infinite depths life has sprung
In myriad forms, known and unknown--
Blessed am I, Midwestern landlubber,
To have experienced your re-creative presence
In Florida, its rivers, lakes, and offshore seas
Revealing the kaleidoscope of creatures
At home in them.

On Saint Johns River, near Palatka,
That manatee family moving so placidly,
Youngsters and oldsters alike, over
The grazing fields under our fishing boat;
At Sanibel Island, those windrows of seashells,
Exotic in shape and color, shared with all
Its neighboring shores by the sun-dimpled sea;
Down in the Keys, from Largo to Key West,
Waters teeming

With a phantasmagoria of tropical and game
Fish, mussels and clams and oysters, lobsters,
Crabs, and living corals. Specially memorable
For me, amateur snorkeler: being unexpectedly
Graced by multitudes of blue tang in silvery
Waters, wheeling, whirling, as one, over, under,
And to the sides of me. Or that encounter with
(And strategic retreat from) a flotilla of barracudas
On territorial patrol;

Or coming upon a dense pack of spiny sea urchins,
Among them that little, glassy, spider-like being
Which broke, then broke off from my bloodied
Forefinger gingerly touching it. And then there was
That moray eel in its coral nook off Long Key,
Its maw opening, closing, before my wary eyes;
And I finally seeing it as only, in its own way,
Breathing, in and out, the breath of life
Crucially needed.

Shell Collection Being Broken Up

The squishy animals once within
Are gone, only their exo-
Skeletons remain, diverse in
Form and beauty; they too must go,
Freely surrendered, gladly given,
To an eager class of Montessori children.

For all my spirituality
Of subtraction, though--
More simply,
For all my letting go--
I've kept a few shells for instruction
And my own contemplation.

Like *Stellaria solaris*, from waters off Cebu:
"Sunburst Star," large golden disc, and rayed,
Spiraling to a cone; it's a "Carrier" shell, too,
With shells and shell fragments arrayed.
Or *Latiaxis mawae*, exquisite mini-pagoda
From Japanese waters; thence, *Argonauta*.

Hians, too, Paper Nautilus' baby-crib; then
Nautilus pompilius, Fibonacci sequence at its best
Revealed in the spirals of my bisected specimen.
From waters southwest of Taiwan comes--modest,
Straightforward, unabashed--*Penicillus penis*;
And from the Moluccas, fluted *Harpa nobilis*;
Lastly, *Murex palmarosae*, from the gulf tween India
And the northwest coast of Sri Lanka.

Shells & Geography--& Marine Biology--
& Ecology--& Cultural History!
Conch & triton trumpets in ritual ceremony!
Shells of all sorts in wampum economy!
Strings of pearls gracing feminine beauty!
Scallops & mussels, oysters & clams, in gourmet cooking!
Molluscan fluids for killing pain, for respiratory healing!
Shells, shells, shells!

O the oceanic reverberations
And celebrations
Of shells!

Practice Makes Perfect

I'm imperfect, you too?
So there's at least the two
Of us. Don't tell Matthew--
He's the tax-man, you know, who knew
Jesus and heard him saying, "Be perfect,
As your heavenly Father is perfect."   Mt 5: 48

Evangelist Luke
(By a providential fluke?)
Has one and the same Jesus
Calling every one of us
To be *compassionate*--   Lk 6: 36
To lend a hand and let

Another know we care.
And though it cost, we dare
To do the works of mercy.
If we practice them faithfully,
Who knows we may one day be
Perfect--by God's mercy.

Matter from the Heart

> Words, words, mere words
> no matter from the heart . . .
> —Troilus and Cressida, V. iii. 108

To heed the Bard, our words are useless, empty,
Unless they're filled with matter from the heart.

And then there are no bars on what our hearts,
Discerning to say and do what truly matters,

Can do with words as we empty ourselves
Into them—and the silences between them.

Pale imitation of the ardent self-emptying
Of the Word made flesh. Still only when

We too enflesh our words do we then
Rise to the heights of the matter
Of being in love, deeply in love.

```
          BENEDICTUS BOOKSTORE
             408 SOUTHLAND
          LEXINGTON, KY  40503
             859-368-0584


  1   979837933155
        Kaleidoscope:: Mirrorin      17.00
                      Sub Total      17.00
                      Sales Tax       1.02
                      Total Due      18.02
                            MC       18.02


                         Change        .00

_____

        Signature - HATTER/CAROL


MasterCard ****2605
PAX   Approval # 21911Z     Chip
PAX   Reference # 317017664011
This Transaction #  1203556
**** Reprint ****
JUN 19, 2023 12:45  1 - 4


              THANK YOU!


           WWW.BENEDICTUSKY.COM
        MAY GOD BLESS YOU ABUNDANTLY
```

Riding out a Nightmare

Chicago's Century of Progress, and I,
four-and-a-half, entranced by the robot dinos
along the Midway as they pluck the hats
off men's heads and (to hoots and hollers)
swoop up the skirts of the young ladies . . .

High in a rocket cab of the Sky Ride--
at night--snapping power cables--sparks--
smoke--fire--shouts--screams--mega-volts
surging through metal and flesh . . . cold
sweat . . . dark, narrow corridor . . . at its end
a strip of light under O the kitchen door

opening to warmth. And the aroma of coffee
freshly brewed; and dad about to leave
for work: Dad, who sets before me a bowl
of warm oatmeal and milk, all the while
murmuring, "It's all right. It's all right."

In Memoriam

Mother, my mother . . . Looking back, I see,
to my sorrow, I took her for granted.

At birth, I almost killed her, tiny in frame;
I, nine-plus baby pounds of me, reluctant
to leave the sheltering warmth of her womb.
Add to the account all her years of living
the "little way" of loving care.

Year after year, the washing, drying, ironing;
all the years of shopping, cooking, cleaning;
the teaching by living word, the preaching
by loving example. And never stopping
to count the cost.

She had her special gifts. She made home
feel homey with her embroideries. With her
soft melodious voice, she sang the Slovak lyrics
she learned at her mother's knee, the family
canary chiming in.

She never could deliver the punch line
of a joke. For cards she had no time, often
pestering dad to leave the table and his buddies.
Her stories began with Adam and Eve,
and then meandered--

"I'm getting there!"--with no real plot or climax.
She didn't like the limelight, preferred to be
backstage, in the shadows. In her little world
she received but little applause. She was,
and is, in good company.

Ideals and Realities

Ralphie, in "A Christmas Story," idealizes
The gift of a popular bb rifle for Christmas.
To his dismay, he hears from his mother's lips
The atavistic cry of every realistic mother,
"You'll shoot your eyes out!" His father, ah!
The Old Man, idealist supreme, enters
One puzzle contest after another, dreaming,
Always dreaming, of one day winning the grand prize.

And one day he does. It comes, in a crate marked
"Fragile"--so it comes from Italy no less!
On being opened, the crate reveals, cradled
In straw, a lamp; a table lamp whose lengthy stem
Is one long, curvaceous, fishnet-stockinged leg--
Platonic Idea/Ideal of all feminine legs!
Perfect for the table next to the front window
So neighbors can see it light up the world!

Ideals and realities. O to see in the light-hearted
Story of Ralphie and family the ideals and realities
Of *The* Christmas Story, in the light of which
Ralphie outgrows guns of toyland fantasy.
And as for fishnet-stockinged legs, yea! Christ
Still plays in tens of thousands of places,
Lovely in limbs not his.

Storytellers

"A story, tell us a story!" so Sis and I,
Many a once-upon-a time ago. And dad,
Carpenter by craft, storyteller
By inner calling, would then begin.
Or more exactly, he'd tell again the stories
We children heard umpteen times before,
And loved to hear him tell once more.

Stories of Janosik, the Slovak Robin Hood,
And all his deeds of derring-do until,
Betrayed to the lords of Liptov, he died,
Hanging from a hook piercing his ribcage,
Defiantly puffing on his faithful pipe.

Dad himself, at twenty-three, crossing the wintry
North Atlantic in steerage aboard *Melita*,
She of the one funnel--always that one funnel
(Unlike TITANIC'S FOUR!)--bringing home
To us that being little can be good, very good.

Stories of villagers who fought and fell
In the Great War; and country burials,
With sounds coming from graves; stories
Of Christmas caroling, Carnival reveling,
And Maypoles. And how he courted Mom.

Teller of stories, Dad. Somewhere between
That blind poet recounting, in grand
Hexameters, the exploits of Achilles
And Ulysses; and that Carpenter of old,
Talking of people walking upside down
In a topsy-turvy world, Dad, with his stories,
Showed us how to live, and walk upright.

Church and Synagogue

They stand out, those two statuesque women
Gracing the south portal of Notre Dame Cathedral
In Strasbourg. Tall stands *Ecclesia*. A queen's
Crown adorns her head; she looks straight
Forward, her royal robes falling in graceful folds
To her feet. In her right hand she holds her cross-
Surmounted scepter; in her left, drawn to her breast,
The precious cup her Son drank from.

Opposite her stands *Synagoga*, slightly
Stooping, her unadorned head inclined
To the side, her eyes blindfolded. But O
How simple and beautiful her gown, also
Falling in graceful folds. And her hands, too,
Are full--a broken lance in the one, tablets
Of her people's precious law in the other.

Their relations in history have been tense,
Yet the one without the other makes no sense.
Together, time and eternity they span,
Fulfilling God's covenantal plan.

Gothic
(In sapphic form)

Not your gloomy novels, like *Frankenstein* and
Dracula, but temples of God that rise on
Pointed arches vaulting in space suffused by
Spectra of sunlight.

Space revealed as sacred; diaphanous-like
Stone. And stained glass glory with gemstone glowing.
Notre Dame * and Chartres; Amiens and Rheims and
Bourges; Cologne and Lincoln and York: the lucent
Spirit of Gothic.

Graced with flying buttresses, great cathedrals,
Notwithstanding gravity, skyward soar, their
Choirs greeting those who are open to seeing,
Seeing light, voluminous light, embracing
Even the shadows.

* A number of medieval Gothic cathedrals are dedicated to
Mary under the French title of Notre Dame ("Our Lady").
The most widely known is the cathedral of Paris, heavily
damaged by the collapse of the iron spire during the fire
of April 15, 2019. Precious medieval stained glass windows
survived the flames and the collapsing stone vaults.

Subjects Fascinating and Elusive

She raised a lot of eyebrows, that February of 1913
At the Armory Show of avant-garde art--she,
Marcel Duchamp's *Nude Descending A Staircase*.
For classic tastes, she was outlandish: a posturing
Cubist abstraction of a naked female body seen in
Frozen motion, simultaneously seen from diverse
Angles. For Pete's sake, women do have curves!

Ah, boundless Spirit at work in the artist.
Kaleidoscopic fragmentation inviting a second,
A third, even a fourth look--yes, from different angles--
Stirring up prickling memories of nubile beauty
Artlessly about. Duchamp's nude may well frustrate
Aesthete-voyeurs but by God she'll grace where-
Ever she is, thanks to a seer's distinctive seeing.

Like Picasso's cubist composition *Demoiselles d'Avignon*;
Or (magnanimous Pablo!) those earlier clowns of his
In classic-figurative pose, and always blue, even
In his rose period; or his torturous black-on-white
Guernica; or those serene, African-inspired
Masks in his later years. And then there's Claude Monet,
Painting and repainting those haystacks in the fields

At Giverny after the harvest; or the Gothic facade
Of the cathedral in Rouen--Monet, painting it
At different times of the year; at dawn, at noon,
By star-lit night, seeking to express on one canvas
After another, simultaneously at times, his fleeting
Impressions of light illumining his subject,
Phenomenon at once fascinating and elusive.

Good Old Cowboy Movies of Yesterday

Years before John Wayne and Randolph Scott became
Stars, while Tom Mix and Bill Boyd's Hopalong Cassidy
Were lighting up the silver screen, my Uncle Emil loved
Westerns. The "oaters" needn't be A-fare; they only had
To go easy on the killing, especially between cowboys
And Indians. Nor did it matter who the actors were--
He did like Andy Devine and Gabby Hayes for comic
Relief. And he didn't mind the wisecracks about more
Horses' rears in cowboy
                     flicks than horses.
He had come to Chicago in the 1920s, leaving behind
A village tucked into the Little Tatra foothills. A horse--
If there was one--was a plow animal; riding it bareback
Was a no-no. So, newly minted American, there he'd be
(Before he married Aunt Martha) in the local Roxy,
Enjoying on a weekend afternoon a Western, usually
The second feature of a twin bill; the main attraction
For him was the combo of rugged manhood, desert
Scenery, and especially,
                   the horseflesh. Horses!
And now I can see why. Mustangs, broncos, ponies--
In great thundering herds, in fluid motion, nostrils
Flaring, manes and tails flying. Stallions, rearing high
On their hooves. Mares, foals, fillies, colts, skittering
About, snorting, neighing. And no matter that most
Of the critters had no names. When technicolor
Arrived on the scene, artists' dreams of equine hues
Found their film palette.
                 Kaleidoscope of coats, manes,
Tails, and points. Blacks, whites, silvery grays; bays,
Chestnuts, buckskins; pintos and palominos; grizzles,
Sorrels, and roans. But enough of memory lane!
Some of the oaters are still around, a welcome break
From the stuff on today's big (and little) screens:
Cold, dark, metallic-robotic conflicts featuring
Enigmatic, inter-galactic forces.
                 Tom Mix, Hopalong,
Andy and Gabby! Keep riding high in the saddle,
Bring back the sunrise and light up our lives!

Where in the World Today

Rome was a where for Troy's Aeneas fleeing
War before Roman fought Etruscan long ago;
There he found safety from the Grecian foe
Avenging a fellow Trojan's philandering.

Italy--a where for flight from northern climes,
For German Goethe seeking *dolce vita* below,
Drinking in the sun, glowing in lemons' glow,
Rejoicing in the finest Tuscan wines.

Where is the where today, in these our times--
Francis, Pope, echoing Francis, *il Poverello*--
Where people will to unite and sing *Laudato
Si'*, resounding Nature's rhythms, rhymes?

Cosmic Symphony Finale

With piccolos and flutes; strings, brasses,
And woods; with the clashing of cymbals
And pounding of drums, let the earthly
Symphony proceed, played by a multi-
National orchestra.

Given the tenor and tone of today's world,
No longer in tune with music of heavenly
Spheres, note be taken of a special request
To rouse the audience. In the final movement,
Let the chorale

Sing, not a crescendoing joyful finale,
But a "Hymn to Sadness," accompanied
By contra bassoons and bass drums, pounding,
Thundering, chords of disharmony, dissonance,
Discord.

Writing in the Sky

It was a day to remember, a day celebrating
Greatness, with thousands massing along
The broad avenue.

Innumerable flags and banners, adorned
With stars and stripes, fluttered in the breezes
Of the sunny day.

Troops in units of stern array, each unit
Marked by uniforms distinctive in cut
And color, marched

Up the avenue, toward the nation's capitol.
Interspersed between the ranks of troops
Were the heavy military arms--

Tanks, howitzers, missile launchers, and
Top-secret atomic weapons--all tools of war
Made for making peace.

The juggernauts thundered up the avenue
To the cheers and applause of the spectators.
And O the military bands!

Blasts and blares of trumpets and bugles,
Pounding of drums, punctuated the pomp
And circumstance. Aloft,

In the sky opposite the pageantry below,
A skywriting biplane intricately maneuvered,
Leaving behind

The name and symbol of greatness in red
And white and blue mists of smoke,
Quickly fading away.

God's Serio-Comic Jester
(Gilbert Keith Chesterton)

Like fellow Brit and apologist Hilaire Belloc--
"Where'r the Catholic sun does shine,
There's music and laughter and good red wine"--
Chesterton enjoyed dining with others, quaffing
Wine or ale with gusto: *Benedicamus Domino!*"
He relished even clerihews, that goofy, lightly
Spoofing form of twentieth century English verse,
Convicting evidence of his sense of humor.

In his serious work as writer and lecturer,
He had a flair for divine comedy, lighting up
Christian cult, code, and creed; and a keen wit
That honed paradox on cant-cutting paradox.
The donkey in his eponymous poem may well be
"The devil's walking parody/on all four-footed
Things" but what a marvelous jackass it is,
As it hee-haws its paean of praise and thanks:

"One far fierce hour and sweet/there was a shout
About my ears/and palms before my feet."
Some other G.K.C. bon mots: "Christianity hasn't
Failed; it hasn't yet been tried." "The whole
Modern world has divided itself into Conservatives
And Progressives. The business of Progressives
Is to go on making mistakes; of Conservatives,
To prevent the mistakes from being corrected."

Then there's the theme on which *The Times*
Of London invited Chesterton to contribute
An essay: *What's Wrong with the World?*
And his one-liner by way of reply: "Dear Sirs,
I am. Sincerely yours, G.K. Chesterton."
To end with his zinger in *Orthodoxy*,
Fingering the humorless and once high
Flying ace of angelic squadrons: "Satan fell
By the force of gravity."

Writing Things Down

Even in these advanced electronic times,
With all their latest obsolescing gadgetry,
Some of us old surviving dinosaurs are still
Content to write things down, for purposes
Of reference, memory, whatever.

But why write things *down?* Instead of *up?*
Or *up and down*, as do (or did) Chinese?
Or *upside down*--naturally, of course,
With all the appropriate gymnastics.
What are these "things" we write down?

They're special things--they're words!
They take on all sorts of forms and functions.
Here and now, let's pay honor to the things
Called nouns. They're mostly common, but some
(Needed to sign our checks) are quite proper.

As infants, we began learning and vocalizing
These noun-things, as we pointed to the things
Pointed out by them. In early school, we traced
Their letters, as we learned to write; in this way,
Adding to our oral way of communicating.

How noun-things written down enrich our lives!
Without them, we couldn't write or read; we'd be
Cut off from arts and sciences, from crafts and trades,
From life-sustaining ritual and story. Awesome
These things, however common. Terrifying,

Their absence in states like amnesia or Alzheimers.
Yes, they can be used for ill; but that's another
Matter. In any case, we just can't take for granted
These "things" pointing to things. Consciously
Or not, we show respect for them whenever we,

Pencil or pen in hand, notebook or paper scrap
At hand, bend our necks and bow our heads--
Perhaps at times even kneel--to write things down.

Words Our Interim Abodes

Words--their sounds, accentual or tonal, trace
Back to primordial shrieks, grunts, and groans.
Their diverse written or printed forms are linked
To ancient wedges chiseled in rock; to ideograms
Painted on plaster or clay; to later alphabetized
Inscriptions inked on parchment or papyrus.

Amazing things, words. Those past, gifting
God-alone-knows how many languages long
Gone, like those who used them. Words still
Around, survivors, but meaningful only
To scholars devoted to them as they lie,
Soundless, entombed in dusty, learned tomes--

Their epitaphs, dumb reminders of those
Who once lived, loved, and died by them.
So, whatever our active and passive vocabularies
Are--all hail! All hail parents, teachers, who
Gifted us with them! In the English-speaking
World, all hail Merriam-Webster, Oxford

International, and Peter Mark Roget!
All hail those who, graced by the Primal Word,
Have helped us learn and weigh our words;
Thus enabling us to build--and for all our
Babel proclivities--humbly, cooperatively,
Rebuild the interim abodes in which

We live and move and have our being.

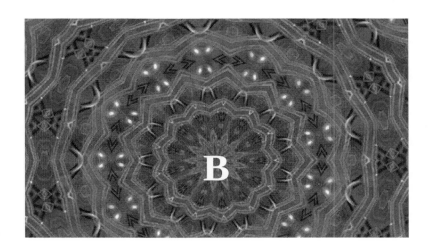

B

Matters of All Sorts that Matter

Out of Sorts--Nothing Matters

> You withheld sleep from my eyes. I was troubled,
> I could not speak. I thought of the days of long ago . .
> At night I mused within my heart. I pondered
> and my spirit questioned.   --Ps. 77

Hermits, monks, nuns suffered from it, still do;
Ancient, medieval, and modern spiritual guides
Warn against it: *acedia*, "noonday devil,"
Apathy, lethargy, sloth beyond sloth--nothing
Happening, nothing mattering, everything useless,
Meaningless, b-o-r-i-n-g.

You don't have to be cloistered to experience it
Today; witness Bill Murray in "Groundhog Day."
You come home from work; from the office, plant,
School, whatever--glad it's all behind you.
But there "it" is, before you: the same darn
Old everything.

That wallpaper in the kitchen--for years
You've thought of changing it to something,
Anything, but different. Then there's the frig
With its rusty hinges; you stare, stare, into it;
Shut the door, no taste for left-overs, too early
For a cocktail, alone.

A familiar wave of ennui sweeps over you;
You feel you are, at best, living (if you want
To call it living) a life of quiet desperation.
Trapped, no way out. But that includes, I hope,
"No way!" to do yourself in. You're not going
To call it quits.

For the kids' sake or for your reputation
Or simply not to disappoint the folks you feel
Do care for you. Usually. And so, you'll try
To grin and bear it. But that hairy itch still
Remains: What's the use? In the end, does
It all really matter?

Gravity

Why so grave, Old Buddy? It can't be gravity.
That gives us earthlings heft, saves us from floating
Off into the void of space. Don't even folks
Overweight have moments of levity?
So down with the grave!

Take a slow, deep breath--in/out--("Come, Breath
Of God, come!"). And appreciate all that comes
With having both feet firmly planted on good
Old terra firma. There'll be time aplenty
For what's beneath.

Phantoms

No, not from ghoulies, ghosties, imagined things
Going bump in the night, not from such fictions
And infantile fears rescue me, Lord.
Deliver me instead from dreaded shrouds
Of memory. Memories of injuries,
Injustices, to me, by me. Memories
Of healing words unspoken, promises
Not kept, and deeds not done. Lord of the tomb,
From phantoms of the past, present like pain
Of limbs no longer there, deliver me.

What's the Matter? A Patient's Perspective

You begin to see things differently
when, having lost prostate and bladder,
you lie flat on your back
for days (and nights) on end.

You see the surrounding world going on,
around and around you; doctors making
their rounds, nurses (God bless them!)
working around the clock;

night shift techs waking you
to check vital signs; and all those
good people--so essential--bringing
fresh laundry or taking the soiled away;

delivering meals and mail, cleaning rooms,
and so on, and so on. And most of all,
you see others are in charge; and you,
until discharged, the O so impatient patient.

Out of Breath

Leisure—the spelling is tricky enough; the matter
Itself, elusive for those seduced by the spell "Time
Is money, spend it well." Consumerist economy,
"Enriched" by technology's latest fads, spins
Its will-o'-the-wisps for people to pursue end-
Lessly. No time for real re-creation. For sabbath
Rest. People out of breath.

Treading a treadmill, even at top speed,
Where does it get us? Up to us to learn how
To slow down, take a deep breath, hold it in,
Let go--cycle of life, matter of divine love,
Acknowledged and lived intentionally.
The proverbial turtle still wins the race,
Beats the fits-and-starts hare.

Let's face it. Earth, for all we've done to her,
Outmatches us in speed, as daily she spins
Around her axis, annually around her sun.
Like St. James' farmer, we can learn patience
From this our amazing Gaia; from her sequence
Of seasons, the organic inter-play of her life-
Giving powers, not to mention

The kaleidoscope of her known and as yet
(Pace Linnaeus) unknown kingdoms;
And the still prevailing cycle of her birth-
Death-rebirth. To crown all this with a variant
Of the American watchword "Haste makes
Waste," there's that anonymous Amish farmer's
Zinger of a zinger: "The hurrier I goes,
The behinder I gets."

Sparrows at the Bird Feeder

Late-evening TV program brainstorming
The chaos on our southwestern borders--
Throngs of unaccompanied children amid
The homeless masses seeking refuge--
With much proposing
                              and counter-proposing
By the opposing parties. Before retiring,
I dimly recalled a quote from Chekhov's
The Cherry Orchard: many remedies
Prescribed for an illness suggest no cure.
The next morning,
                              I passed by the bird-feeder
In the garden and its primary welfare
Recipients--the sparrows, congregating
And in flitter-flutter bursts of passerine
Energy, taking in seed, then taking off
For their nests, singly or
                              in little flocks
To feed their fledglings.

Tenting Tonight

Perryville, site of unhappy memory:
The 1862 fraternal battle--Bragg vs
Buell--over precious water running short . .

This autumn evening, men and horses rest,
Content with the quiet before the conflict
To be reenacted in coming days. The chill

Of falling night is tempered by the warmth
Of lanterns lit within tents that flicker
Like fireflies up and down the slopes

Surrounding the extended countryside.
As battle duels go, compared with Gettysburg,
Fredericksburg, or Chancellorsville, Perryville

Is nothing to brag about. Not counting
Horses (and mules), the casualties numbered
A little over 7,000; about 1500 perished.

Visiting a Bluegrass Breeding Shed

Her back protected by a leather apron,
The mare awaits the coming of Himself,

Winner of the Arc de Triomphe at Longchamps,
For years now sire of champions, prize stallion

At stud, with millions at stake. Attended by
A retinue of equine vets, stable hands

And the farm manager, the thoroughbred
Descends upon the arena, surprisingly

Not a stamping steed snorting fire
But a smallish bay at best fifteen hands high,

An aging Caspar Milquetoast of a horse
Clip-clopping to his designated post

Behind the mare. He mounts her, finishes
His business, is led away. "Third one

For him today, like every day," pipes up
The manager, "and two months counting."

Ace in the Hand vs Uncivil Religion

Offputting, those male and female evangelists
Praying with earnestly screwed up faces.
Granted, the man prayed over needs it
In view of his self-pitying cries and all
His messianic make-believe.
                            He's dealt
With scary avatars of evil. Hard to believe
He'd kneel for much of anything; he does
Stand for vigilantes of the self-appointed
God-and-country kind; and he likes to have
Them standing by--
                high-risk stakes, playing
With the Great Divider. Vaunting an all-knowing
IQ and pelagian all-doing, he disses critics.
Those who won't play his game, he forgets
Not nor forgives. One faithful follower of his
Admits the man has a dark side;
                       but he too--
Given the millions still giving their allegiance
(And millions) to the man and his cause under
The bright white banner of American Greatness--
Would vote for him, were the ex to be re-invited
To occupy the White House.
                 Sad state of affairs
For the grand old party once led by Lincoln
At a time crucial for the Union, its sheer
Survival at stake. But in a saying linked
With Abe, we have an ace in the hand (not up
The sleeve!) to trump
               the self-acclaimed master
Of the art of the deal at his losing game
Of uncivil religion: "You can fool some
Of the people all the time, all of the people
Some of the time, but not all of the people
All the time."
          And then there's the party-
Transcendent line crucial for our time,
And echoed by Martin Luther King Jr.:
"The moral arc of the universe is long,
But it bends toward justice."

It Really Matters

Ever been in a funk--nothing matters?
A give-away, that "matters." Were we angels,
Purely spiritual creatures, the question would be
Immaterial, of no concern to us. But let's
Let angels be.
                (It takes one to know one.)
So back to us "funk-ables": what's the matter?
We are! We're matter spirited or, if you will,
Spirits embodied. Lots to chew on there.
"Spirit" is tough enough; and "embodied"--
Well, that brings up
                  all sorts of bumpety-bumps
And proverbial rubs. We fall physically,
Weighed down by our bodies, subject to gravity;
We fall spiritually, uprising in our adamitic flesh.
But--praise the Lord--our original fall
In Genesis is not
              original. It comes only
After God's luminous words for material creation:
"Let there be light." Matter is called forth
From darkness by God, holiest, purest,
Of spirits; and pronounced good. Amazingly
More. God freely,
              lovingly, brings human
Matter upon the prismatic cosmic scene;
Makes it the matrix of the eternal, co-equal
Son's self-emptying into finite creation --
Jesus the Christ, born of the Virgin Mary,
God incarnate.
             Still more! Jesus' enfleshment
Becomes the crucible of his passion and death
On behalf of fallen sinners: mystery of love
Beyond all telling, climaxing in his resurrection--
Mortal human nature now raised to heights
Sung by the angel choirs.

                              So to play down
Matter or to take it for granted is bad enough;
To condemn it as intrinsically evil is blasphemy:
Christ--on trial for godliness before Sanhedrin
And Empire--is for his fleshliness despised
By every gnostic Manes.
                              Yes, matter matters;
It does take its toll. We're not angels;
We're not Superman or Spider Woman either.
We're human, at times all too human bumpety-
Bump beings never fully at rest here "below,"
Never in full control.
                              Still it would be childish
To cower in a corner with a woe-is-me
Unbeatitude. Blessed are we when we open
Our eyes and see ourselves through the eyes
Of fellow-embodied Jesus: not prisoners
In a cave, doomed
                    to shadowy darkness,
But people of hope. As every Twelve-step
Program attests: it's amazing what people
Can do when they face up to themselves,
Accept a helping hand, and together walk
Into the light.
                    Amazing, as in grace!

Ice Storm

(Lexington, Kentucky; Feb. 16-21, 2003)

Crystalline branches crackle and crack,
Shower down in frosted shards; limbs scud
Through the air and hit the ground with thuds;
Power lines down, transformers blown,
Light and heat--utilities ordinarily on hand
With the flip of a switch--wrenched now
From thousands of homes and businesses
By a gelid fist.

Stress on necessities: food and medicine
Delivered to the elderly and shut-ins;
Generators installed in public shelters;
Home-amenities reduced to sponge baths,
And simple meals prepared on the gas-top
Kitchen stove--while battery-run radios
Regurgitate news of preemptive fire-storms
In Baghdad: "Shock and Awe!"

New-found priorities: felicity of fire
In the hearth, with stories and laughter
Over hot chocolate and s'mores; silences,
With reveries of flickering tongues
Heralding the rise of phoenix-worlds.
Then, as the hush of night descends
And revelers retire, time to find oneself
A restful nook; there, inspired

By the warmth of glowing embers,
Pen oneself a heartening poem.

Crossfire

(July 1997)

"NO!"
      LAST
           NIGHT

From hundreds at the candlelight vigil
On the grounds of the governor's mansion
In Frankfort, Commonwealth of Kentucky;
Hundreds gathered in peaceful protest of
The killing-to-be of Harold McQueen,
Who killed young Rebecca O'Hearn
Seventeen years before. McQueen's execution,
By electric chair, part of the common wealth,
Is to be the first in our State since 1962.

Our governor, an honorable man
By democratic standards, has heeded
The *vox populi* and signed the death warrant.
Some legislators, forward-looking, are
Looking ahead to change--to change
The legal mode of killing
From electrocution to lethal injection,
From frying victims' brains to filling their veins
With venom. More humane, say the experts.

I missed that candlelight vigil--
An emergency call brought me instead
To the side of my sister-in-Christ Ellen,
She of the eighty-seven winters,
Lying in a hospital bed in Lexington,
Soothed by sacrament and morphine,
Dying of burns from a fire started
By a fallen votive candle in her shrine
To Mary. Ellen went home to heaven

YES
      TER
           DAY.

Iron

Element Fe: by mass, most common metal
On earth, present in stars as well, highly
Malleable. In the hands of Promethean
Man, forging ahead in the Iron Age
With his dreams of unending progress,
Iron, fired with diverse alloys, hardens.

Corporate towers, buttressed by steel, loom
Over the tenements below. Armor and sword
Turn into cannon and shell. Ships, once of wood
And canvas, pass from ironclads to vessels
Of steel from keel to masthead, titans
Imposing their sway over the seven seas.

A compass in a ship of steel--massive metallic
And magnetic forces throughout--risks pointing
Not to its primeval and primal cynosure
But to its metal confines, and so imperiling
The steering of the ship in course and heading.
And one day even dreadnoughts will rust away.

Will Homo Sapiens (whatever his gender
And age will then be), be wise enough, humble
Enough, to look up anew to the heavens
And navigate by stars and their soft light?

American Tanka Threnody

how far we've fallen
blest son   Walt   of Manhattan
from your visioning
this land as a sacred land
venturing and hopeful land

how far we've fallen
from keeping our doors open
to the homeless poor
be they   Asian   African
or non/north American

how far we've fallen
producing   selling   weapon
on weapon for war
when   no war is civil   when
we trust not God but Mammon

how far we've fallen
from compassion   the golden
virtue you upheld
toward both kin and alien
toward the many and the lone

how far we've fallen
from your   *Song of Myself*   rhythm
of the unique I
in union with all that's on
this Earth   and with all   beyond

Blasphemy

In the beginning
At Alamogordo   "*Trinity*"
Name of uncreated mystery
Name for a new creation now
With its promethean creator
Stealing elemental fire
From heaven   uranium
In fission   genesis
Of Bomb A

New primeval fall
Vast conflagration
Outsunning the sun
On the Day of the Son
Feast of the Trans
Figuration   the Day
Of the One   Light
From Light come
To become one
With us   for us
To become light
And salt and yeast
Rise to overcome
The Beast

And on that August Day
Came from the womb
Of *Enola Gay*
In the name of the US
Of A   *Little Boy*   entombed
Among us

The Comedy, December 2000

on this the third
millenial eve
of the common era
unoriginal
sin going back back
far back
to the adameve

dantesqueries
mortal and venal
commissions
omissions
by major and minor characters
a comic troupe
playing the Inferno

on a cosmic stage
continuing
conflagrations and expurgations
with who knows what
surprises and
revelations
at the falling curtain

Live and Learn, Learn and Live

(Villanelle)

By ups and downs of life, as time flies by,
The wise among us learn and bear in mind
We die a thousand deaths before we die.

Our best laid plans so often go awry;
Our visions, dreams, and hopes are left behind
Through ups and downs of life, as time flies by.

The goals achieved don't fully satisfy,
And family members, friends, move on, remind
We die a thousand deaths before we die.

Amid success, our failures testify
We have our bounds. We find ourselves confined
By ups and downs of life, as time flies by.

Along the way, we barter or deny.
We flee or fight. Resisting or resigned,
We die a thousand deaths before we die.

To live and learn, to learn and live, defy
The gravity that holds us down. Refined
By ups and downs of life, as time flies by,
We die a thousand deaths before we die.

Facts as a Matter of Fact

Foundations once destroyed, what can the just do? --Ps. 11

Facts facts facts   so much depends on facts vs fake news
As a matter of fact
Oceans are choking
Forests are burning
Mountains are melting

Wake Rabboni wake
Wake Rabboni wake
Winds are howling
Waves are towering
Wake Rabboni wake

As a matter of fact
Border walls rise high
Unparented children cry
White nationalist flags fly

Wake Rabboni wake
Wake Rabboni wake
Winds are howling
Waves are towering
Wake Rabboni wake

As a matter of fact
Blacks don't matter
Vigilantes gather
Politicos blather

Wake Rabboni wake
Wake Rabboni wake
Winds are howling
Waves are towering
Wake Rabboni wake

As a matter of fact
Wars for peace end with tombs
Kids are killed in classrooms
Childrentobe in mothers' wombs

Wake Rabboni wake
Wake Rabboni wake

Fable of the Great White Wannabe

Once upon a time, in a land this side of the sea,
Arose a great white Wannabe. With promises
Of progress, production, and pride, he drew
To himself multitudinous disaffected ones.
And day and night he tweeted alternatives
To the news he in his Greatness proclaimed
To be fake.

The greatest of his Good News was his being
The peace-maker the world was waiting for.
And so, at his command, wall upon wall
Arose for the nation's internal security.
He multiplied its weapons of war for making
International peace. Venturing farther out
Into the unknown,

He created a Shiva-arm for arming space.
In all this, he, great white Wannabe, had
His eye on one man, a Black man, a man
Who won the Nobel Peace Prize, although
(So Wannabe) the man did not deserve it--
Unlike him, the Pelagian do-it-all.
But one day,

Breaking news broke through the illusions
And delusions of his Greatness. Thousands
Of his disciples whom he had commanded
To stand by were surging now in wave on wave
On the nation's capitol, storming its barricades
And walls, beating back its outnumbered guards,
Desecrating its halls,

All the while flourishing Greatness banners.
Amid the din and confusion, the great white
Wannabe himself was whisked away,
Ending up in the House called White,
Heedless of facts unrolling, history
Unscrolling.

Membership Card from the
National Rifle Association

Arrived in the mail, unasked for, a card
Two-by-three-and-a half-inches, plastic,
Pitch-black background on both sides.

On the back side, at the top, a white
Strip for the member's signature; below,
Also in white, a sacred text noted: the Bill

Of Rights, Amendment II. On the front side,
To the right, big white figures announce
The Year of the Lord; to the left, the round seal

Of the NRA glitters in gold. At the bottom,
Also in gold, shines my embossed name--and two
Long numbers; clearly, I'm more than just one.

Quite fitting, given the growing numbers
Of people killed by guns empowering them.
I'm keeping the card to remember, and remind.

Darkness from the East

Israel--Palestine, Palestine--Israel:
Vicious old circle, impossible to square.

With the Sinai, twin Peace Nobelists Begin
And Sadat began to think outside the circle.

Nobly daring, too, Arafat, Peres, Rabin,
Braved stormy waters, hoping, always hoping

The dove from the ark will circle the sodden
Earth and find a perch among the olive trees.

New millenium now; Obama, new Peace
Nobelist, deploys drones in a widening arc;

Wannabe Nobelist Trump, in the name of Dis-
United States, unilaterally, with great pomp,

Decrees the Golan Heights in Syria belong
To Israel, and Jerusalem is Israel's capital--

To the anger of Palestinians everywhere
And the dismay of nations fearing anew

The rise of the fascist cry: Make (you name it)
Great Again! In the mean time, corpses on

Corpses throughout the Middle East feed
The ravenous beaks circling overhead.

Darkness of Cover-ups

Men in blood-red robes process,
Blind-folded, up the center aisle
Past others buried headfirst in sand-

Boxes along the walls, their legs
Twitching above to the tempo of
Ecclesiastical rock; while alone, off

In the shadows, *alter*
Christus, another Christ
(O Christ!) defiles a child.

In the ongoing mean time,
In the sanctuary of the chancery,
Sealed and hidden documents,

Rotting with the smell of Judas,
Remain lost from the saving light of day,
Lost for the victims of the night.

Princes of the Church

Pomp and circumstance clerical,
Presumptively ecclesiastical;
With sources Constantinian,
Byzantine, and Carolingian--

All too ambiguous legacy
Imperiling the scent of sanctity:
Good shepherds humbly smelling
Of their sheep. A bishop dubbed "Bling"

Spends millions on his residence
And loses every measure of credence;
Another revels in his vestments
And episcopal accouterments:

An imposing miter almost twice
The usual size; albs trimmed with finest lace;
A *cappa magna* of crimson satin
Trailing yards behind him in procession;

Also a gem-studded golden ring
And pectoral cross--thing upon thing
That for Christ dying, naked on a cross,
Would be so much dross.

Survival Skills

How can one survive the depths of hell,
How survive humanity become inhuman?

Viktor Frankl, Austrian Jew interned
In three Nazi concentration camps, among them
Auschwitz, retained his sanity and *survived*
By virtue of his nascent logotherapy,
With its stress on finding a meaning for life
In order to meet life's challenges.

Maximilian Kolbe, Franciscan friar, Pole,
Interned in Auschwitz, held dear to his heart
The memory of the One who, from Nazareth
To Calvary, gave his all for a new creation,
Giving good Father Max good reason for him,
Too, to lay down his life for another.

Love! Bonding Covenant Old and New!
Frankl, in Auschwitz, came upon the *Shema*
Hidden in the rags he inherited from one
Sent to the ovens; in its light, he found
Strength in the memory of his beloved wife,
Parents, and brother, all holocaust victims.

Love, there in Auschwitz, there in Frankl's
Own barracks, in the persons of those few
Internees who shared their meager rations
Of bread, breaking off fragments for those
Companions starving even more than they--
All starving for love.

"Little Certainties"
(In Sapphic Form)

Nietzsche's madman clamors, to scathing laughter,
"God is dead!" And buried with God are all our
Vaunted values, absolutes--Earth now lost in
Cosmical darkness.

"Little certainties"--in those concentration
Camps sans reason, one needed counting: one plus
One is two, and one minus one is nothing.
One is of value.

Nietzsche, too, that day on that street in Turin,
Fearful night about to befall him, rushes
Forward, warding blows off that hackney nag, in
Fearsome compassion.

What Do You Do With Dead Soldiers?

Who won't stay dead?
You bury them
Again and again.
And again they rise

In arms, march off
To war--and die,
Divisions on divisions,
World without end.

What do you do
With dead soldiers
Who won't stay dead?
What do you do?

What   must   we   do?

On Converting Swords into Plowshares

When swords have been at last converted
Into plowshares, will the former swordsmen
Know what to do with them? Has anyone
Shown them what fields are, beyond battlefields?
Or how different they can be, and how different
The ways of cultivating them? The whole
So-called order of a disordered society needs
To be restructured. In time. Lots of time.

Time! Measure made up of many moments,
Each moment a Now, a present, a gift. Even
An "eternity" of time would still be time,
Continuum of change in terms of before,
During, and after; with the old giving way,
Time and again, to the new. "Giving way to":
Not the violence of bloody revolution
That sees no good whatsoever in the past,

And sows the seed of future discord.
Instead, pro-ceding from, growing from,
Outgrowing the seeding moment past:
Evolution, antonym of devolution, humans
Engaged in the differentiation.
Over countless eons, from the Adameve
To the present age, Earth has seen her children
Coming upon the cosmic scene;

Capable of destruction but also of metanoia,
Conversion of mind and heart: turning away
From swords and battlefields, turning to vines
And vineyards, and cultivating them; putting
New wine into new wineskins; then peacefully
Sitting down at table among the fruits
Of their common labor. And, all together,
Enjoying them.

Hardships Launched in the Thousands

("Operation Iraqui Freedom" 03/19/03)

Trojan elders, sitting in the shadows
Of the city-walls, admired Helen
As she passed by in the fragrant aura
Of her beauty. Paris, her paramour,
They cursed for his twin hubris of blindly
Biting into the apple of discord
And stealing Helen from Menelaus' bed,
Bringing her to his.

Today, dalliance far more epical.
In ancient Iraq, men and women, thrilling
To prospects of liberation, curse
The occupiers from abroad, now
Embedded among them, espousing
The hubris of "Shock and Awe," blind
To consequences.

Family Movie Run in Reverse

Moving backward and out from Pentagon
And White House offices, Generals,
Cabinet Members, and the First Man
Converge aboard Air Force One, flying
Tail-first, at Mach speed, through the dust
Swirling in space from bygone empires;
Then descending, still tail-first, landing
At dawn in the Adameve, and taxiing beyond
To a prehistoric gorge where, jet-disgorged,
The wary arrivals, backs to what's ahead,
Look around for pre-emptive rocks.

Christendom vs Christianity

Christianity: Failed? Never tried! (after G.K. Chesterton)
Christendom: Christianity without soul (after Christopher Dawson)

division
excommunication
power plays
crusading ways
pride and hate
of church and state

by Shakespeare eyed
exemplified
theist vs atheist--nay
faithful vs infidel--nay
Yea! Catholic Henry V
vs Catholic Charles VI!
Saint Crispin's Day--
Hip-hip-hooray!
Henry's band of brothers
has its francophobic druthers

Victory!
To English Glory!
Swift and pure
at Agincourt!

union
inter-communion
humility
charity
common fall
brothers and sisters all

no longer lost-deemed
but grace-redeemed
with Jesus' Spirit on mission
and end-time commission
to re-create earth and heaven
be the new Christ-leaven
raising
a world gestating--
all this
to the honor and glory of his

beloved Abba   lingering mystery--
why Jesus let Judas be
at the first bread-breaking then even
in the olive garden . .

Games People Play

In the current
Context of the holocaust *Ukraine*,
Apocalyptic echoes of the cold war
Recur: "All options are on the table."
And then, there's game
theory: "If X,
How many millions, compared with Y,
Will suddenly perish?" "And if Z,
Is it Earth's zero end-game--in cosmic
Skies a momentary
burst of brilliant light,
Planet Earth and everything on it reduced
To molten radioactive rock?" In the meantime--
Time more and more mean--is Ukraine,
With forty million plus
(not minus, of course,
Children), the sacrificial lamb offered up
By worldly powers desperate to avoid
An otherwise inevitable World War III?
Ukraine--Ex? Why?
How long before Z?

The Three Theological Graces
(After Peguy)

Theologians (who should know better)
Abstractly call them "virtues," with the bias
They're somehow virile. But Faith, Hope, and Love
Are wonderfully feminine, more graceful
Than even the Graces of classic Greece.

To start with the mature one of the three:
Love, wife and mother, symbiosis
Of Mother-Earth and Mother Courage;
Homemaker, seamstress, baker, cook--the gift
That keeps on giving, there where she's needed.

Faith, maiden in her budding teens, winsomely
Shy, coming to know and be more sure
Of herself, trusting in the power
And benevolence of the life-blood
Pulsing in the depths of her being.

That leaves us with little *Hope*,
Precious infant issuing forth into a world
Of precarious time, precarious space,
In a burst of water whose hidden source
Flows from eternity to eternity.

How Ignatius of Loyola Ruined Me for Life

Yes, he did it, Ignatius of Loyola,
Under God, my spiritual father.
He took hold of me, naive, vulnerable
Teen just out of high school; through intense
Spiritual exercises he helped me hear
Jesus calling me (me!) to join and work
In his company,*
                              never counting the cost--
A work-ethic in no way the worldling's
Get-ahead-at-all-costs. Just get this:
Those spiritual exercises not only
Inspire desire to share in Jesus Christ's
Redemptive mission in a suffering world;
They also entail a corporate ideal:
To advance in following
                              Jesus, God's Son
Become human, by striving to become
More and more like him--poor, humble,
Obedient to God no matter what; yes,
Even hated, maligned, unjustly condemned
And killed, a fool in the eyes of both secular
And clerical powers. Donald Trump,** vaunted
Master of the art of the deal,
                              where were you
When Ignatius of Loyola ruined me--for life?

* Company (or Society) of Jesus: founded by Ignatius and nine fellow
  companions; approved as a Catholic religious order by Pope Paul III
  in 1540. "Spiritual Exercises": (1) prayers, meditations, devotional
  and ascetical practices; (2) title of Ignatius' manual originally noting
  his personal experiences of the foregoing; later editions expanded and
  published for the use of spiritual directors and directors of spiritual retreats.

** Controversial entrepreneur and ex-president of the United States;
   Cf. American haiku: non-magnanimous
                              was he chose to keep tabs on
                       all his quid pro quos

A Matter of Identity

Jesuits--God's Marines! The first to hit the beach!
So the legend I once thought was true. *Semper
Fi*--ready to charge, and die. The macho image
Found its sonic reflection in the way American
"Jebbies" of an earlier era sang the hallowed
Company song, "Take, Lord, receive." You felt
The pounding beat, sensed the adrenalin flow,
And glowed with honest pride.

Then came the "flowers in the gun muzzles" era
Of the '60s; and the St. Louis Jesuits with their
Rendition of the song, once so martial, now
A tender love song--to the raised eyebrows
Of older Jesuits and their lay cohorts.
Back in '46, our novice master counseled us
Teenagers just out of high school and the "old"
Vets of WWII to cool any gung ho bravado.

Desires, holy desires? Yes! Under the banner
Of the cross and in service to God's kingdom,
To desire to know, love and follow Christ,
Not counting the cost. "Honor flashed off exploit?"
Even among US Marines there's honor
In standing watch at the White House doors
Or around a catafalque in the Capitol
Rotunda. As for Christ--Savior of the world!--

He spent nine-tenths of his brief earthly life
Hidden in the boonies of Nazareth.
What good has come of it? If nothing else,
The toughest discipline for gung ho types:
They also serve who only stand and wait.

A Housewife's Heavenly Extravaganza
(Luke 15: 8-10)

Let's get this straight. A thrifty woman,
Pride of her husband, loses a debit card
With the full balance of $200 on it.
Retracing her steps of the past few days,
She looks everywhere she can think of.
She finally finds the card under a pillow
On the sofa in the living room.

She calls and e-mails her friends to come
Later that week and celebrate with her.
She in the meantime prepares a party
To end all parties--costing over $2000.
Well! (But let's keep this on a heavenly
Plane and not worry about her hubby
And his reaction.) Extravagant? You bet.

Nay more--out of this world! After all,
It's Evangelist Luke's inspired take
On Jesus' magnanimity; on his exuberant
Joy over anyone once lost but now
Found. And yet even that good news pales
In comparison with the wondrous fact
That he, God's Son enfleshed, died

So you and I might live.

Ten Virgins and a Wedding Party
(Matt. 25: 1-13)

Ten virgins came to celebrate a wedding,
Ten virgins with lamps, five of them foolish,
Not bringing oil enough to last thru the night.
And a long night it was proving to be.

The groom and bride delayed their coming.
When finally they did arrive, only the five
Wise virgins were there to greet them.
The five foolish virgins had gone off

To buy oil for their lamps gone out.
No wonder the welcoming scene was less
Bright, fewer welcomers present for what
Could otherwise have been a gala event.

From a human perspective, it's sobering
To note the five wise virgins didn't share
Their oil with the foolish ones. Granted,
In the worst-case scenario, the lamps

Of all ten virgins would go out. Surely,
In that event, the groom, good man, would not
Condemn the wise for their kindness. Oil is,
After all, only oil. People count, people matter.

And people in darkness can still sing together,
Can't they? And even dance? Or is there
A darkness so thick and so impenetrable,
And the dancing hall so big and unfamiliar,

You just can't orient yourself? You (and your
Partners)--you're lost.

The Hairy Ones and the Smooth-Skins

We'll never know for sure if it ever was perfect.
From what has been pieced together from stories
around the fire, things began to go sour
with Smooth-Skins distancing themselves
from Hairy Ones.
                        At first, Hairy newborns
would nestle against the hirsute females
suckling them; but shortly, babies ever less
hairy began baring their toothless gums
and screeching at their witless nurturers.
Smooth-Skin children
                        howled and hooted
as they chased Hairy adults rapidly retreating.
Existential rifts grew wider as Smooth-Skins,
armed with their weapons of wood or stone,
rounded up Hairy Ones, male and female,
young and old;
                        they forced even the sick
to work: gathering wood, tending the fires,
skinning the kill, cooking, cleaning up--all
exclusively for the benefit of the Smooth-Skins.
Post-puberty males also used Hairy womanfolk
for sexual relief, pleasure.
                        The worst abuse
occurred the day a number of Hairy children
at play died, victims of a fire. The smell
of roasted flesh aroused the Smooth-Skins;
they tore into the crisp and charred remains;
licked blood and bones;
                        sucked out marrow
and--voracious appetites unsated--looked around
for more to devour. It was then (per rumors
from the past) surviving Hairy Ones descended
upon their oppressors. With the untamed fury
of their ancestors,
                        they killed every Smooth-Skin
around; took whatever they could carry off,
weapons included. Then they disappeared
into the surrounding forests, never to be seen
or heard from again.

Shall We Gather at the River?

There once was a land with a beautiful river,
Like the land, alive with life. The sun
Shone on it by day; the moon, by night.

But then, the unimaginable happened.
Upriver, where the mass of the population
Lived, the waters were turning red.

People were coming to the river,
Under the cover of clouded moonless nights,
Singly or in whispering groups.

They were coming with things wrapped
In rags or hidden in boxes. Their numbers
Grew. And they now came openly by day.

Downriver, people, horrified, tried to save
What they could of the things floating amid
The ordinary flotsam and jetsam.

Still others went upriver to see for themselves
Who was throwing the things into the reddening
Water. And why? They came back, their moral

Compasses askew in view of what they saw
And heard. Arguments over what human rights
Were . . .Which and whose rights were at stake . . .

Whether the things thrown into the river were
Human or not. . . Whether a woman has a right
To do what she wants with her body. . . Matters

Of property rights . . .etc. etc. Or as a cynic
Might say, ad nauseam. But the river is still
Running, still pharaonic-red.

Postmortem Agenda

What do you do,
vanquisher or vanquished,
with burnt-out, bombed-out,
villages, towns, cities?
With all the rubble
of big and small buildings
littering shell-pocked streets;
with the remaining floors
of partly standing ruins
exposing daily intimacies,
toilets, showers, beds, precariously
tilting outward toward the voids
of walls protectively once there?

The rubble of ruins does have to go
somewhere, carried away, hauled away,
to be--when possible--recast, remade,
rebuilt; or, when impossible,
ultimately--in ashen, atomic, or
other elemental form--
buried. But what
do you do when, in trying
to bury the rubble,
you disturb, upturn,
graves of uncounted dead?

Much Ado about Important Matter

To give or not to give? Covid vaccines,
Made from cell lines of two fetuses
Aborted in the '60s--now available
To be given for life. Yes, but *taken*
From life, at the cost of life. So all
Depends on who the taker-giver is.
Is it Frankenstein?
                           Or is it Rachel?
The *Baron*, grave desecrator, lab
Idolator, labored to create life
In his likeness, and to control it.
His avatars today, equally foolhardy,
Concede no reasons to tread lightly
Where others in the field may hesitate
To tread at all.
                           In contrast, Rachel mourns,
Still mourns, her children killed by Herod
In many guises. And yet, woman of faith,
She puts their fragments in vial-reliquaries
For reverent remembrance. And more.
With forward gaze and higher, selfless intent,
Rachel looks up to the innocent Infant who
Survived Herod;
                           who out of sheer love
Gives us his vulnerable manna-flesh
To be ingested, consumed--for our health,
Our growth, our life. Enlightened by this
Vision of fleshly communion, Rachel--
Questioning pilgrim on her Emmaus way--
Finds her way free to release those vital
Fragments from their vials.

Spirit-Matter of Fidelity Cut to the Quick
(Consolation in Desolation)

Hard to believe--Teresa of Calcutta, model of selfless
Service to the poorest of the poor, suffered decades
Of spiritual desolation. Day in, day out, she'd be
Out in the city, succoring abandoned infants,
Attending to the sick and the elderly, praying
With the dying. But her life
                              of service to the poor--
A life involving her confessor-approved vow never
(Under the pain of mortal sin) to refuse anything
Jesus asked of her--took its toll: a self-questioning
Down to her most engaged and existential depths.
That gentle, smiling face she projected to the world,
Was it a fake facade hiding
                              a life of make-believe?
The misery she encountered there in Calcutta, where
And how was Jesus there? Did she really believe
Calcutta was her way to holiness--a matter of Jesus
Loving Calcutta's poorest of the poor; she in turn
Loving Jesus, no matter how dire the circumstances?
Or how meager the fruits
                              of all her labors?
This ongoing, profound self-questioning became
For her the time-hallowed ways of spiritual
Purgation and illumination leading to her union
With Jesus--Jesus, dwelling in her; the Jesus
Of the garden of Gethsemane in St. Luke's
Unique account:
                              crying out to Abba
For help; *sweating blood--and an angel*
Appears beside him. No mere angel, this.   (Lk. 22: 39-46)
Not at this momentous hour when humanity's
Fate, yes, that of the whole cosmos, is at stake.
Consolation in desolation--no sweetly singing
Bluebirds, no sweet-scented lilies,
                              no rising suns.
Instead, the Holy Spirit, Twin-Paraclete, Consoler,
Advocate, there beside the faithful One on the way
To Skull Hill and the new creation beyond.
In her Calcutta/Gethsemane, Mother Teresa,
Woman of fidelity cut to the quick, was--is!--
Truly in great company.

Breathing/Venting: A Matter of Spirit

(In Times of Desolation and Consolation)

In the nethermost pit of Dante's hell broods
Satan, frozen up to his waist in a lake of ice,
Alone, wordless. His wings (two pairs, gigantic)
Beat the sullen air, generating a bitter wind
That winds its way up to the entrance.
There looms the warning: *Abandon hope,*
You who enter here.

Here "below" as well? Desolation? Hell
On earth? In itself, it's neither sinful nor
Morbid. It can become a deep freeze of mind
And heart, where nothing grows, nothing
Matters, and one feels terribly alone. God?
Silent . . . Ah, Desolate One, take heart.
Accept the gift of time,

Each moment a present. Take it. Make it
Your time, and breathe it slowly in, slowly
Out. Take time also to find an Other you trust.
Seek her or him for "direction"--spiritual
Companionship--grace upon grace for you
Confiding, Other primarily listening; both
Engaged in ongoing discernment

Of things that matter; things of the meantime
(Mean things included), things of the end-time.
Two fellow pilgrims on the way--with Jesus
Sooner or later joining in on the conversation,
Never without his Paraclete Twin.
In the holy exchange, a letting go occurs,
A letting out--a *venting,*

Precious grace, in times of desolation,
In times of consolation as well. *Vent,* then,
Companion on the Way! And keep on *venting,*
Be it by cry or sigh, stutter or groan; yes,
By moments of silence, when heart speaks
To heart. *Vent*--from the Latin *ventus,*
Meaning *Wind.*

Our embodied spiritual venting,
With breathing as its vital airy transport,
Is unique both in its finite human being
And in its infinite divine source. It rises
From our depths--depths enshrining
The Holy Spirit. In God's good time,
Our breathing and venting

Become a graceful synchrony of thanks-
Giving to Christ's Spirit: Comforter,
Counselor, Breath of God, Paraclete-Twin,
Present in our hearts with warm-warm wings
And light, refreshing breeze.

Fragment like me Confine the Almighty?

Or limit the Spirit, lilliputian i?
The Spirit breathes where Spirit will,
In whirlwind and wave, in noise and still,
Even in passing whisper or sigh.
A brook rippling day after day
Over the stoniest rocks wears them away.

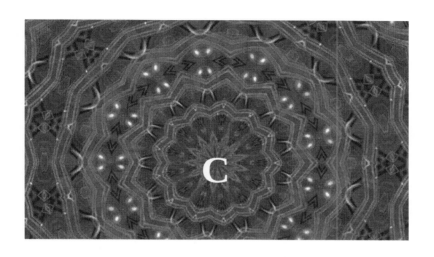

All Manner of Things
That Matter Will Be Well

Matter Mysterious

Sing a new song to the Lord . . praise his name
with dancing and make music with timbrel and harp.
--Ps. 149

Matter mysterious

Creation contingent
By divine
Design
Made permanent

Freely
Lovingly
Made super natural
Indispensable

For love to be
Embodied
Crucified
To rise and be

The new creation
New Earth   New Heaven
God All
In all

Spirit and Matter glorious

God with Skin and Spirit (Like Us)

Charge it to God Father, accepting the Son's choice:
The way of the flesh. Not coarse carnality, but en-
Fleshment, whereby the Son, born in time of Virgin
Mary, took on bones, blood, nerves, muscles, and skin--
To mention mentionables.
                    We have God's word
For it that Jesus on earth was like us in everything
But sin. So, tempted? Yes, and pace Kazantzakis
And Scorsese, we can let our imaginations cool off
And face further facts. Jesus, tempted, didn't sin;
We, his fleshly kin, do.
                In fact, since the Adameve
And its raw originality, we fallen mortals aping
One another are a bathetic harlequinade
Of ugliness and folly. But along with the skin
In which we prosaically sin, we share with Jesus
His Paraclete Twin,
             the Holy Spirit, Ruah--
Breath of God . . at work in cosmic creation . .
At Jesus' conception . . in those hidden years
Of his youth . . in his public ministry.
And definitively present at Christ's side
In the twin ordeal
          of his temptation
In the garden and on the cross. By him
In the tomb, breathing him back to life, new life!
Christ risen--his own mission on earth fulfilled,
He leaves his disciples; leaves them to the Spirit
Empowering them
            to witness to, and realize,
Christ's Good News of a new world. Now, in this
Our time in the end-time, Christ's Spirit is our
Ruah, breathing on us, born anew in the waters
Of baptism; cleansing us of pore-clogging sin.
Our Paraclete: counseling,
            encouraging, us
In our mission: to breathe new life into a breath-
Less world; to set it afire with pentecostal tongues
Of ardent love; to undo Babel's divisive cacophany;
To usher in a new creation where, on God's word,
All will be well.   Very well   shall it all   be.

Ode to my Legs and Feet

I sing, old Buddy, of the legs and feet
That, thanks to you, are mine. In infancy,
They helped me to discover and explore
A world where everything was new--and tasted
Good, even though Mother didn't think so.

Dad, proud first father that he was, creator
Also of my cradle, how he encouraged me
To take my toddling steps toward him and fall
Into his outstretched arms. And as the world
Turned round and round, I also got around

More and more, outgrowing cradle, outgrowing
Everything Baby, becoming Boy. And boy-o-boy,
How these legs and feet of mine came into play!
To run after a ball, climb trees; to skate and swim
All summer long; and then, in autumn, return

To school, chase after girls, learn how to dance,
Learn how to stand up straight, walk like a man;
Walk across the stage, receive the coveted
Diploma, mom and dad proudly beaming.
Commencement! A new beginning, with all

Kinds of courses, leading to the choice
Of a walk of life and walking it.
Old Buddy, you and I know the details,
And how the devil was at times in them.
But the walk has been basically good.

Now, as it slows down and age creeps up,
We have time to pause and feel, bare-footed,
The silken grass; time, still time, always the gift
Of the present, to keep on walking ahead
Into the receding horizon, hopeful, always

Hopeful, in case of storm, to be, like Peter
The Fisherman turned Rock, to be able
To walk, even on water.

Old Buddy

Plato made you the prison-cell of soul,
And even gentle Francis nicknamed you
"Ass" (tho he softened the tag with "Brother").
For over ninety years now, and still counting,
You've helped me live. As hair and teeth fall out;
As hearing, sight and other senses weaken,
And even physical desires ebb,
I realize how much you mean to me,
How much I've taken you for granted--

You and the wonders you've revealed to me
In the expanding horizons of my life
From infancy to age. So, Old Buddy,
With what remains of us, and in the time
Remaining, let's try, you and I, to be good
To one another, patient in suffering,
Enduring losses, grateful for every gift
Anticipated or unexpected, always, in every
Way, open to more wonderful surprises.

Birdsong at Night

Late on a night in spring I listened to
A lone mockingbird at the garden edge,
As it charged into its solo repertoire,
Mimicking whistles and peeps, trills,
Chirps and chirrs, off-key, loud, non-stop,
Repetitive, the hour I stayed to listen.

I parted with pensive memories of another
Spring night, years before and a continent
Away; the night I first heard a nightingale
Burst forth in melancholy echoes of melody,
Reminiscent of Melpomene, just paces
Away from me in the forest.

Its rounds of sound suffused the darkness,
Followed by moments, longer or shorter,
Of silence; and at varying intervals,
From nearer or farther away in the wooded
Depths, resounded song on wistful song,
Nightingales responding.

Fall Meets at Keeneland

Splendor
Of color:
Mums,
Geraniums,
Oaks and maples in full array;
And on prominent display,

Pennants, flags, banners,
The colors
Of these
Rivaled by the silks of jockeys;
While their mounts' tails, manes,
And coats of diverse shades
Gleam
With a special sheen,

As if to show
Nature here below,
Proud of her place
In the race,
Is out to win
In

A blazing spree
Of Bluegrass glory!

Fall Prayer While Raking

If leaves could feel falling and, falling, fear;
And if I myself were only a leaf
Clinging to one of these oaks or maples
Rustling in the autumnal wind, I too,
With trembling kin, would fear a chilling fall.

But human as I am, Lord of the leaves
Enthroned on a tree, I praise and thank You
That all about me shades of summer's green
Fall, luminous with beauty, transformed
To vermilion-gold, warmed by the harvest-sun

ABCs of a Vowed Celibate

I began to be
in ways beyond
my memory
                    A
            in the dark warm womb
            of Woman
            on earth
            my birthing mother
                    B
            and since my birth
            I've never been
            as deeply in
            another

sans memory
of A or B
and in answer
to an inner
voice I've freely
vowed to be
                    C
            celibate for life
            without a wife
            yet not alone
            but one

            with and in
            Christ human
            and divine   with sight
            of faith   looking

            one day to being
            in *Communion*
            with all within
            the Triune One

new beginning
without ending
All-Wombing Light

On Zeroing the I

In the word *live,* ponder that i--it has
great but latent potential. So much
of the time i is weighed down by ego.
To be free, free to take wing and soar,
i must venture to rise above ego--
only to find time and again that ego
and i are one: the self-centered self
unwilling to let go.
                    But in time, series
of Now upon Now, gift of the Ever-
Present, ego/i can learn to surrender
itself, die to itself; by no means thereby
annihilated, reduced to nothing.
Instead, poor little self, opening out
to ever widening horizons, outgrows
its self-ishness, me-me-ness. Enriched,
i becomes uniquely,
                    gracefully, I:
distinctive human Self, in communion
with other Selves, all called to be in union
with I Triune. True, I, rising from ego/i,
undergoes self-emptying . . selflessness . .
darksome 0-ness . . But the i in live
is--grace upon grace!--rounding out,
transforming to o, crucial O, making all
the difference, in time
                    and for eternity.

The Monk Who Raised His Voice in Laughter

Tom's laughter was open and honest and spontaneous:
what was so refreshing about him, what made his face
light up, his eyes actually twinkle.
--Ron Seitz, *Song for Nobody*

The man of Tao/Remains unknown. And the greatest
man is Nobody.
--Thomas Merton, *The Way of Chuang Tzu*

Thomas "Tom" Merton--Father Louis--
What's in a name other than the one
Given us by the One beyond
All naming, One who calls
Each of us by name?
Better to be
"Nobody"
And leave to time
And eternity our growth
Into our God-given name.
And then--for all the caution
Archived in an old monastic Rule:
"Only a fool raises his voice in laughter"--

To laugh, laugh, as if our lives depend on it.

The Gift of Laughter

> Blessed are they that laugh at themselves,
> for they shall never cease to be entertained.
> --Chinese proverb

That baby boy, just bathed and powder-dried
By Mother, now being dressed and hugged
And kissed by her--how that bouncy little being,
In all his innocence and trust, giggles
And laughs, graced with the gift of laughter.

To laugh, laugh, always with others, never
At others' expense; to laugh even when things
Don't go our way or when we only play
Second fiddle; yes, to laugh when we fall
Flat on our prat--grace upon grace to be able

To laugh at all, lightening the load of being
Human, for all its gravity. In contrast
To Lucifer, once upon eternity most luminous
Of creature spirits; Lucifer, who (if rumors
Are true) took the splendor of being angelic

Far too gravely, looking down on God
Scripting and playing the divine comedy
Of mortal flesh; Lucifer, Light-bearer, who fell
From heights of heaven into infernal darkness;
Lucifer, who lost the lightness of being.

Jesus Laughing, *Pace* Chesterton

Jesus in my office, laughing; I mean *laughing*!
Head thrown back, mouth wide open, eyes
Crinkling with mirth. No way the Pantocrator or
The Man of Sorrows! All-American Ultra-Lite?

Certainly not Chesterton's cup of tea.
In his *Orthodoxy*, he makes the point
That Jesus, in the four canonical Gospels,
Never laughs. So, no sense of humor?

For GKC something far deeper is at stake.
Jesus, in the hiddenmost depths of his incarnate
Being, has a divine gift that he, out of compassion,
Keeps secret: the Holy Spirit's gift of joy.

The Spirit by whose power Jesus was conceived
Of Mary; the Spirit, who gracefully hovered
Over him as he grew in age and wisdom,
Feeling a deepening kinship with key figures

In the sacred scrolls--Suffering Servant, Paschal
Lamb; then, in Jesus' all too brief public ministry,
The Spirit at work in his twin-paraclete's depths,
Quietly helping him divine the day to come,

When justice, tempered by God's mercy, will be
Served; and all will be well. But in the meantime,
Jesus himself is loathe to appear in any way
Indifferent to injustice, suffering, pain.

He conceals his sanguine joy but in word and deed
Reveals his compassion. And yes, Chesterton's Jesus--
In an early poem ante-dating his pre-Catholic
Orthodoxy, laughs. But he is all alone, high

On a mountain peak, at night, "under the terrible stars
In stern array/casting down their sharpened spears."
In that cold, bleak, and lonely darkness, Jesus laughs.
Pace Chesterton, let's change the scenario along lines

Of fellow Brit--and rollicking cradle Catholic--
Hilaire Belloc. Change it to Jesus, early at dawn,
Beside his beloved Sea of Galilee, fishermen
Bringing ashore their bounty. Jesus, heartened

By Ruah, prays to his Abba. The sun rising,
Jesus' eyes begin to twinkle; he smiles, breaks
Into a laugh, his laughter resounding amid
The olive-green hills and over the sparkling sea.

Artists and Clowns

In tone if not in color Picasso drew
his clowns and all their family members blue,
even in his rose period. The hu-

man comedy limned by the Artist's hand,
for all its song and gaiety,
is charged with pain and frailty.

Rouault's Christ-Harlequin would understand.

Goodness/Beauty: *Fecundity*, Motherliness Divine

Goodness/Beauty--luminous deity dimly seen
By Plotinus, ancient Neoplatonist moving beyond
Plato's heaven of eternal, unchanging Ideas
And his world-cave
                  of ever-changing shadows.
Newly seen by Friar Bonaventure, venturing
Onto the field of faith seeking understanding--
Seeking to see divine goodness and beauty
In the light of revealed Trinity:
                  eternal community
Of tri-personal Love. To see, within Love-Trinity,
Abba "Father" unbegotten, but begetting, first
Among equals; philosophically to baptize and name
"Him" *Fecundity*: fruitfulness,
                  self-giving Love
That keeps on giving--spontaneously affirming
The Son's eternal emanation, and eternally exhaling
The Spirit. Moving "outside"/"without" the Trinity,
To see the uni-verse coming forth,
                  freely, out of Love
Overcoming nothingness. Kaleidoscope of creation--
Dazzling finite, fragmentary reflections of all-loving
Goodness/Beauty mirroring one another; all integral
And conducive to
                  the goodness/beauty
Of the cosmic whole. Still more to see! The Son,
Creative-iconic Word, himself becomes a creature,
Eternally desirous thereof; becomes a vulnerable
Baby in Virgin Mary's womb--
                  matter of love,
Sheer love, fecundity upon fecundity, now graciously
Human-divine! Jesus accepts suffering, dying. Rising
From the dead, he raises fallen creation; with manna
Immortal, he nourishes
                  his body of companions
On the narrow way; confirms them with his Twin
Paraclete; commissions them to revive the breathless
World as, in joyful hope, they look forward
To Goodness/Beauty,
                  rejoicing with her reunited
Children of all times and places at heaven's banquet--
Fecundity, exuberant Love beyond all telling.

Prayer with Saint Augustine

Mystery,
Nearer to me
Than I to myself, open

My eyes, loosen
My tongue in prayer,
Praising your grandeur.

For woe to the silent
When even the eloquent
Are dumb. O ancient Beauty

Ever new, deliver me
From the seduction
Of your creation

Seen apart from You. Set on fire
My restless heart with ardent desire
To turn away from idols; to turn, turn,

And find my rest in You; to burn
With love of You loving me--never
Too late! Giver

Of grace upon grace,
Grant that I see You face to face.

The Kiss

(American Haiku Sequence)

two pairs of lips meet
entreat each other to let
one another in

their innermost hearts
sanctuaries of being
not alone but one

with one another
in times good and times not good
but in God's good time

time to be the two
beyond themselves one with God
in life eternal

Consummation Devoutly Wished

(In Memory of Dr. Jim Holmes, 1941-2007)

my friend   for you
as for me

final revolution
around the sun
over and done

with escape velocity
on to a new
dimension

and finitude in infinity
finally
be

The Day Before My Father Died
(February 14, 1973)

St. Valentine's Day. That afternoon, he bought
His gift for mom: a big, red, heart-shaped box
Of chocolates; he gave it to her at supper-time,
With a tender hug. Afterwards, at bedtime,
He read his card to her, telling her, first,
In someone else's words, and then his own,
How much he loved her.

The next day, blurred in her memory, she felt
Him leave her side, heard him go and clear
The sidewalks of newly fallen snow. For her
And others. Never finished. "Massive myo-
Cardial infarction," they said. Nothing
(They tried to reassure her) could be done
To save him. As if he needed it.

Anamnesis at my Mother's Wake

Her skin, once warm, soft, and supple,
Cold and stiff now, and oh, so dry,
An ancient parchment scroll, brittle
Under a Dead Sea sky.

But more than arid skin or even marble
Engravement to come, "Here lies . . . ,"
She in her deepest self is incorruptible,
Distinctively survives,

Awaits her final and definitive edition,
To be announced and sung by choirs
Of angels and archangels in heaven,
And saints purified by fires--

While I, here beside her emptied body,
Stand and stumble through my prayer
For the one who in love enfleshed me,
"Remember, Lord, fulfill her."

Dying and that Dickinsonian Fly

she puts out light lines
that go deep   pulls up lunkers
with minimal tackle

--Anon.

fishing . . . hope, always hope

--Anon.

Angler Compleat, Emily,
Casting her fine-spun lines sounding
Aslant Death's profundity,

Pulls up a fly, ending a story
Of sight out of sight foundering
In the flotsam of memory.

Hope and its allure! Hope that nothing--
From the first Aha!-moment of Seeing--
Nothing, graciously nothing

We pull up in Heaven,
With whatsoever Fly buzzed our Dying,
Will darken our Vision.

Sounds of Silence

(Matt. 4: 1-11; Mk. 1: 12-13; Lk. 4: 1-13)

Hot, very hot, that day in the desert
Outside the oasis-town of Jericho--and I,
Dead-tired from hours of tracing, on my own,
Kathleen Kenyon's excavations of the area,
Multilayers dating back to times unrecorded
But for the stones upon eroding stones.

I never made it to the top of the mountain
Looming over the desert plain. Up there
Hovered the monastery marking the site
Of Jesus' forty days of prayer and fasting
Before encountering the spirit of evil,
Triple-tongued, intent on undoing him.

In the shade of a crumbling wall I took
Shelter, grateful for the bottled water
Quenching my thirst . . . Silence, everywhere--
Broken by only the muted barking of a dog
In a village off in the distance. And the sound
Of a cock crowing.

In the Garden Of Gethsemane

(Luke 22: 39-46)

He could run away, hide. He knows--he feels
It in his flesh--the moment, the Hour, he
Has long expected, has come. And with it,
Darkness and dread.

The figurative Passover he just celebrated
Is past. Now begins the real passage from
Bondage to promise, its bodily fulfillment
In and through him.

Alone--his three companions fast asleep--
He prays, O how he prays, sweating blood;
Prays to his beloved Abba for strength to be
Faithful to his mission.

A momentary respite--his twin Paraclete
Appears in angel guise, consoling him,
Strengthening him, in this crucially pivotal
Moment, to stay the course.

Time in the Edenic garden quickly passes.
Distant, muffled, din; clamor of voices nearing;
A shadow approaches, hovers over him, its body-
Language giving off a kiss--

Password to the Adamitic Hill of the Skull
In the dark valley across the way.

Crucifact

(alt. The Twelfth Station)

Darkness, three in the afternoon,
The air is thickened with flies
And the smell of blood;
The drone of surrounding voices
Is pierced by an agonizing cry.

Nothing new here. Elders have seen it all
Before. Justice, praise God, is blind.
What had to be done, is done.
They've done their part,
Time to turn in for the night.

The centurion and his men will see to it
That all still to be done, will be done
According to the book. Barring
The unforeseen, they can then
Turn in and call it a day.

Prayer before a Monumental Crucifixion
(Gruenewald's Isenheim Altarpiece; Colmar, Alsace)

standing at the foot of the masterwork
i look up at Jesus on the cross
in the central panel

his fingers claw the darkened skies
his thorn-crowned head sinks
low on his chest

the whole of his body blemished by
maculations of the plague
i bow

and silently pray
God my God
what a Man

Celebrating Martin Luther King Jr.

Gathered around the eucharistic table,
Guests of the unique High Priest, uniquely
Just and compassionate, we celebrate
The Reverend Dr. King. Not canonizing
Him, we leave to God the recognition of
His good and faithful servant. To those
Who, constricted by their mediocrity,
Zero in on human weaknesses,
Intent on reducing vessels of clay
To idols with clay feet, we profess
That Brother Martin now bears the wine
Of Jesus Christ in his new-born skin.

Of all the honors we can give him
Within our holy communion, by far
The greatest is to imitate him; to call out
The bigotry that continues to divide
These our "United" States and the world;
To confront the crucifiers in our midst
And counter their hate with love; to feel
The pain of the crucified and share
The pain of relieving it; to keep present
And alive the Reverend Dr. King's dream
That one day boys and girls of all races
Can play and pray together, so that one day

The way of the cross will be ended
And the stone blocking the tomb removed.

Rouault, St. Luke and Emmaus

(Lk. 24: 13-35)

One artist complements the other: Luke
Portrays the scene, Rouault provides a key
Detail. Disciples, two of them--usually
Portrayed in Western art as males, but not
So here--are on their way to Emmaus, one
Named Cleopas; the other, no name, clue
Enough to see in No-Name, No-One,
Another one of those anonymous women
Luke proclaims as part of the Good News.

So Rouault (God bless him) would then be
Right on target, putting beside good Cleopas
A woman. Why not his wife? Why not that Mary
Who, among the women standing at the foot
Of Jesus' cross on Calvary, is identified
In *John's* Gospel as the wife of Clopas?*
Coincidence? Or deeper truth? Woman and man,
Together, lost, disconsolate, questioning,
Searching, open to the Stranger opening up

The meaning of it all.

---

* Jo. 19: 25. There the name is Clopas. Clopas was the brother of Joseph,
husband of Mary, Jesus' mother; the latter was thus sister-in-law of
Cl(e)opas' Mary. See Pablo T. Gadenz, The Gospel of Luke [part of the
series: Catholic Commentary on Sacred Scripture] (Grand Rapids:
Baker Academic, 2018), 394, n.9.

Angel with Two Pairs of Wings

Remember him? Clarence, that imperfect angel,
Angel without wings, in "It's a Wonderful Life"?
Clarence, sent down from heaven to help George
Bailey, who's on the brink of despair. The funds
That were supposed to keep Bailey's home loan
Agency afloat--gone, vanished! On the way to
Being deposited in old skinflint Potter's bank.
And all this happening on Christmas Eve.

George is crossing the town bridge, tempted
By the river below, when Clarence materializes
Before him and jumps into the icy waters!
Spontaneously, George jumps after him
To save him. Clarence's mission has begun:
To save George from himself; to save him
From his hapless wish he had never been born;
To save him by showing him all he has done
For others. None of it would be, if he
Had never been. But he is, they are, and--praise
The Lord--it's still early Christmas Eve.

In George's home, family and friends gather
To greet him before the brightly shining
Christmas tree. At its foot is a laundry basket
Filling up with bills and coins--also present
And pitching in, several bank creditors no less.
Word of George's predicament has leaked out
And folks are ah, so merrily and generously
Responding. To the tune of Auld Lang Syne.

Only a wishful dream--and a nightmare its
Greater part? Love's at the heart of it all;
From-heaven-down-to-earth love, helping
Clarence to win at last his angel wings.
Morally bankrupt Potter wasn't there for
The happy ending. Tough chestnut to crack.
But Clarence, cherubic Clarence, may one
Day soon be sporting a second pair of wings.

Poetic Mystique of Transformation
(Rainer Maria Rilke, 1875-1926)

He leaned a lot on others and could be a drag,
A drone living off beneficent feminine admirers.
But even in their company (or his wife's),
He treasured, *needed, solitude,* inner silence
Enabling him to take in and inwardly process
Things, their happenings;

                 and the joys, sorrows,
Gains, and losses occasioned by things in all
Their be-coming and going. How he desired
To see into things, become one with them,
One day to see beyond their spatial-temporal
Conditioning--epiphanies of a benign universe,
Enduring, perduring.

                His apprentice-years
In Paris in the studio of sculptor Rodin,
And in symbolist poet-circles, prepared him
For his masterly sonnets and elegies--at heart,
Threnodies. Yet their chords were very different
From the nigh-contemporary Dionysian refrains
Of Nietzsche's madman

                 intoning a requiem
For God. Rilke was inspired by Orpheus,
Empathetic hero of myth, demidivine poet
Of love and loss and lyre; Orpheus, forever
Mourning his beloved but O so mortal
Eurydice; Orpheus, singing his love for her
In immortal lyrics.

             And she, Eurydice,
Reappears to Orpheus-Rilke--in the person
Of Russian-born Lou Salome, once student-
Admirer in brief concert with Nietzsche,
Now in romantic liaison with Rilke!
She reveals to him Mother Russia's soulful
Folk-spirituality; and he--

            despite that *Maria*

In his name--rejects "The Sound of Music"
Catholicism of his disaffecteded Austrian
Youth in favor of the beauty and solemnity
Of Byzance on the Don. And yet, those iconic
Russian angels and archangels, aren't they
Open to question as well?
                              Immortal as they are
And radiantly beautiful--awesomely, terrifyingly, so.
Do they, can they, care about us, suffering mortals?
Who of them, in which angelic choir, can identify
With us, answer our cries, or at least listen?
In Rilke's eye, we human mortals are aerial
Beings with a new score
                              for angels to learn
And sing with us, however Earth-bound
We presently are, changing, always changing.
In the light of Andrei Rublev's *Trinity* icon,
Featuring three angelic figures transcending
Race, gender, age--all three robed in splendor
And majesty, and seated
                              around a simple
Serving table--may Rilke, seeker of beauty
In and beyond the fragmentary and ever-
Changing things of experience, find special
Welcome from the middle figure: eternal Son ,
Eternal Icon, eternal Word, who, in wondrous
Exchange, took on change,
                              and on the cross
Made change supra-angelically immortal--
Mysterium tremendum fascinans.

Judging a Copy of the *Last Judgment*

A copy, only a copy, but what a copy,
Marcello Venusti's *The Last Judgment*,
Based on Michelangelo's masterpiece.
The Master himself approved it. It saves
For us what the original
                         was condemned
For: nudes! All those naked bodies, male
And female, saved (to the right of Jesus
Judging) and condemned (to his left)--all
Judged by both Church and State to be
Gross, and so
               doomed to be draped!
Jesus stands there in the upper center,
Risen and judging, both arms menacingly
Directed toward the condemned. He, too, is
Naked but for the sheer fabric clinging
To his loins. Venusti
                 does take liberties.
He adds two figures at the top-center
Of his painting: God-Spirit hovering
As a glowing dove; and above the Spirit,
God-Father, looking upon the whole scene
Approvingly. Let's leave
                 the real finalizing
Judgment to God's infinite justice, tempered
By God's infinite mercy. In the meantime
(However mean it may be), praise and thanks
Be to God, from whom all nudes proceed,
To whom they all return.

Facing the Consequences

(Luke 16: 1-8; and 19:1-10)

On the face of it, incredible--Jesus' parable
Featuring a manager about to be fired
For mismanagement. The man's chutzpah
In what he does to save face is trumped only
By the business-owner's

                  reaction. What's up?
The manager curries the favor of the business'
Patrons by finagling their debts; and he sees
To it that they're aware to whom they are now
Indebted. The owner gets wind of the shady
Dealings. You'd think

                  he'd blow his top.
Instead, he praises the key-shyster--"birds
Of a feather..."? Praises him for his laser-like
Focus in knowing and getting what he wants.
We leave to their just deserts the hell-bent
Minions of Mammon

                and look at another
Lucan business type. Zacchaeus! The little guy
From Jericho, Danny de Vito in toga drag--
And (Lord, have mercy!) a tax-collector.
We see him on a sycamore branch, literally
Out on a limb to catch

                a glimpse of Jesus
Grinning up at him. Coming down, Zacchaeus
Vows to give to the poor half of what he owns;
And he'll quadruple the sum he owes anyone
He's cheated! Jesus, not to be outdone in being
Generous, *invites himself*

                to dinner--God!
What next? must have thought the law-and-order
Pharisees present. So be it. But Zacchaeus
Can now face himself in the proverbial mirror
Without despising what he sees there. And what's
That eating together all about?

                Preview! Wedding
Banquet dimly seen by Isaiah. No more masks!
No more social distancing! People of all sorts
Welcome to the heavenly feast, seated together,
Face to face with one another. And with God . . .

Francis of Assisi, Saint Sans
Arms Lauded by Lenin

Jesus, the diamond with many facets--little wonder
    Canonized saints come in many incarnations.
From Dante's Eleventh Canto in *Il Paradiso*,
    From among the uniquely blessed rejoicing there,
May Francis of Assisi step forth-- *il poverello*,
    The little poor man.

He gave up everything he could to be at least
    A little like God's Son, who emptied himself
Of glory, becoming flesh. In the spirit
    Of Jesus, arms stretched out on the cross,
Francis at the height of the Crusades chose
    Church Vulnerable

Over Church Militant. During the Fifth
    Crusade, he ventured a peaceful meeting
With none other than Saladin the Great's
    Nephew, Malik al-Kamil, finding in him
A welcoming Sunni Muslim, coinstrumental
    In arranging the presence

Of Francis' followers in the Holy Land
    To this day. Then there is Vladimir Lenin,
Atheist, with his encomium. In an entry
    Found postmortem in one of his notebooks,
Lenin writes to the effect: Yes! Tsarist
    Russia needed a revolution; tragically,

It turned out so bloody. "What Russia
    Really needed was ten Francises of Assisi."

Easter Diptych

> Behold, I tell you a mystery . . the trumpet
> will sound, the dead will be raised incorruptible,
> and we shall be changed.
>
> —1 Cor. 15: 51-52

Wombs and Tombs

Dark and warm are wombs,
Aquatic chambers of life--
And they who dwell in them
Emerge one day and see the light.

Dark and cold are tombs--
Will come a day, past strife,
When sightless they who dwell in them
Emerge, regain their sight?

Spring Sabbath
(In sapphic verse form)

Calls of finch and cardinal freshen morning's
breath, announcing winter is past, the frigid,
barren season finally ended, earth now
open to springtime.

Lilacs lightly scenting our garden, coffee
freshly brewing, rise, my beloved, and breaking
winter's fast together, let's listen, wing with
eastering heralds.

Simeon's Twilight Self-Offering

(Lk. 2: 25-32)*

Lord of all left-overs
and over-all fragments
to you I leave all
that I leave undone
or done but partially
the odds not evened
and ends not ended

To you I commend myself
as well   to you and
to your mercy   always
so kaleidoscopically
wonderful that I can
in all ways hope
that in the end all will be

well   all will be   well

*Closing scriptural passage in every day's celebration of the
Liturgy of the Hours on the part of fragmentary Simeons.

Rehearsal

Old Buddy, for many years now we've been
So close together that I can't begin to imagine
Life apart. Before our common act has run
Its course, and the final curtain falls, and theater
Lights are dimmed; before I'm overwhelmed
By the strangeness of the darkened stage,
Or distracted by what is or isn't happening,
I want to take this moment to thank you.

To thank you for all the things you've helped me
See, hear, feel, smell, and taste: indispensable
Matter for all my flights of fancy and
My more pedestrian thoughts. And people,
Ah, the people whom--were I to try acting
Apart from you--I'd never have come to know,
And treasure. Sooner or later, Old Buddy,
I'll have to take my leave of you and go

My separate way. I hope that in the new
Creation of this amazingly prismatic universe
We'll meet again; and, renewed beyond all
Imagining, we'll live anew as one.
Until then, all the best. And blessed be the One
Who has empowered us to be and act
Together. Godspeed, Old Buddy, Adieu.

Leaving the Safety of Shore

Seigneur, in answer to your call,
I leave the safety of shore
And head out for the deep.

Familiar terrain and faces fall
Ever farther behind, ever more
A receding past. I keep

Looking ahead, buoyed by your promise,
"Fellow Voyager, Friend,
Follow me--this

Our common venture,
Will safely end
At the other shore."

More Things in Heaven and on Earth, Horatio

Hamlet I. v. 125 ff.

. . Than are dreamt of in your philosophy. Incredibly,
In the kaleidoscope of mirroring fragments, they all
Matter. Bloody sweat and its stench of fear, marks
Of the lash, a crown of thorns, two beams crossed,
Spike-like nails--yes, they matter.

                    As does the dying
On Skull Hill--God graciously undoing what Man
Unkind has done. It all matters what God continues
To do in and through matter--matter, mysteriously
Real. The deeper we delve into it, the more refined
We find it as it dis-

           appears in infinitesmally smaller
Quanta of energy. Material creation (we have the word
Of God for it) is good. It continues to be God's gift
Upon gift freely given out of sheer love. The kaleido-
Scopic beauty of its various orders is a cosmogenesis
Into which God's Son

           has historically "emptied"
Himself, to quote inspired Paul. Incredible! Jesus
Conceived and born of the Virgin Mary by the power
Of the Holy Spirit. Matter of divine love enfleshed;
Matter beyond science and its domain. And still more
To matter! Mary's womb,

               marking Christ's earthly
Beginning, leads to the tomb; marks his earthly end,
With a new beginning. Once again, it all matters.
The stone blocking the exit, rolled away; the burial
Garments, neatly rolled up, put aside; the tomb itself,
Empty. Too small to contain

              the risen One, now still
Embodied but immortal. Seated at his Father's hand--
Yet another metaphor that falls short of mystery,
Mystery of the real, of materiality transcending
All telling. Horatio, your disquieted and disquieting
Friend still reminds us:

            There are things in heaven
And on earth beyond us, things we can only point to.

Tanka Paean to Matter

> How many are your works, O Lord! In wisdom you
> have made them all . . You send forth your spirit,
> they are created.   --Ps. 104

Of all that matters
It's mysterious matter
Itself that matters
Elementally within
God's order of creation.

Prepared for Virgin
Mary, Mother of God's Son,
Matter matters made
In him-through-him-unto him
Made flesh for our salvation.

Still more! His passion
And death and resurrection:
Our mortal matter--
Renewed in elevation!
Matter in exultation!

Eucharist on the Menu
(Theology of Food 101)

Cornucopias of creaturely delights: foods
On our menus. Fish and fowl, meats, veggies,
Greens, herbs, fruits, berries, nuts spill out
From God's imagination, enticing our senses,
Inspiring chefs, amateur, professional, master,
To conjure up their own culinary creations.

Stop and savor it all: flavors, fragrances,
Oils, juices--God hidden in them for now,
Serving us self-effacingly, giving us
A foretaste of the divine delectability.
But let's pause lest we lose ourselves
Prematurely in heavenly delights.

So, for the present, a memo: that Daily
Special, *Eucharist*. Sacrament, Memorial
Sacrifice and Meal, welcoming us all
Into the mystery of our Savior's Passion,
Death, and--Man Alive!--his Resurrection;
God-in-the-flesh served to us and serving us.

As Lamb, offered for our passover to new life;
As viaticum, our journey food, the final repast
On our earthly passage; as all-gracious host
Of the heavenly banquet to come, the eternal
Present foreshadowed in the gifts of Now.

A Matter of Substance

Do I believe, really believe? So I, standing
Before God's People, briefly distracted;
But in a moment, and in the name of Jesus,
About to breathe new life into the white wafer
And the ruby wine in its golden goblet resting
On the table before me.
                            Do I believe Jesus,
The second Moses, feeding a few thousands
On Palestinian plains and declaring himself
To be the vital bread for countless pilgrims
On the way to life eternal? Jesus, abandoned
By many who find his self-offering hard
To accept. All hail Peter!
                            With him I do
Believe. Peter, who, hearing Jesus ask
His Twelve, whether they too will leave,
Inspired, replies: "Lord, to whom are we
To go? Yours are the words of eternal life."
I thank God, too, for Paul, Peter's fellow
Blood-witness;
                            Paul reminding his flock
In Corinth--and us today--to celebrate
The eucharistic mystery with reverence
And with care for one another. Thanks be
To God also for the faith-witness of Church
Fathers and Doctors--among the latter,
Women like Hildegarde,
                            Catherine, and the two
Theresas; likewise for my parents, teachers,
And all who have opened my mind and heart
To the eucharistic Christ. Eternal Son of God,
Creative icon, in whom, unto whom, all is
Created. All a matter of Love--love raising
Mountains, plumbing
                            sea- and sky-oceans!

Incredible Love, whose taking on our humanity
Is our incredible way to taking part in his divinity.
By comparison with which the mystery
Of the Eucharist is sublime child's play.
Yes, it does take a child--the proverbial
Little one still
                with a sense of wonder--
To accept the glorious gift of the Eucharist.
All hail Peter, aye, all too human Peter,
But Simon made Rock! Faced with Jesus,
Questioner, he replied with his own life-
Seeking question: graced witness of faith
To his standing before and with the Answer.

The Body in the Field Hospital

> All the parts of the body, though many, are
> one body, so also Christ.   1 Cor 12: 12
>
> Husbands, love your wives, even as Christ
> loved the church and handed himself over...
> that she might be holy...a great mystery...   Eph 5: 25-32

Bravo, bravissimo! God-Spirit
   inspiring Paul to acclaim the Body
      of Christ, its members all so crucial

to the goodness/beauty of the whole.
   Virtuoso echoes resound throughout
      Paul's letter-compositions; they come

to their trumpeting crescendo
   in his sublime Ephesians: All hail
      Jesus the Christ, Covenant-Groom!

One with your Virgin-Bride,
   celebrating the wedding banquet
      orchestrated of old by prophet Isaiah.

            *   *   *

Bravo, bravissimo! Pope Francis
   complementing Paul; and, in synchrony
      with the tone of our times, presenting

the church-body of Christ as a field hospital
   in a battle zone. All there--staff and patients alike--
      are wounded healers, called to care for each other.

Presumptuous to wish for a little humor
   in the score? Like M.A.S.H.-- with the light
      notes of zany Cpl. Klinger, the steady beats

of radioman Radar and Father Mulcahy,
   all in concert with old cavalry man, Colonel
      Potter, on horseback clip-clopping happily about!

Angels and the Rider on the White Horse

Then I saw the heavens opened and there was a white horse;
its rider was [called] "Faithful and True. . The armies of heaven
followed him, mounted on white horses and wearing clean
white linen.   --Revel. 19: 11, 14

In Scripture's narrative of God's ways and ours,
Angels and their fallen angelic counterparts
Appear from the start. Adam and Eve are deceived   Gen. 2 & 3
By the Demon-Serpent and exiled by God   cf. Wis. 2: 23-24;
From Eden. Cherubim with fiery swords   Jn. 8: 44;
Then stand by the gates, guarding the way
To the tree of life in the garden's center.   Gen. 3: 24.

The folklore and myth-shrouded tales that follow   Gen.4-11: Cain and
Climax in God's punishment of the hubris   Abel; the Nephilim;
Of the new Noah-generated human race.   the Great Flood;
But that linguistic babble becomes the biblical   God's covenant with
Prelude to a definitively new and infinitely   Noah; city and tower
Far-reaching divine and human intercourse,   of Babel
Via the most extraordinary messengers.

They speak to Abraham and Sarah near Hebron;
To Lot in Sodom; to Job and Tobit; to Isaiah,
Ezekiel, Daniel; to Mary of Nazareth and Joseph
Her husband; to the shepherds in Bethlehem--and
In Seer John's *Revelations* they do much more!   Revel. 4-12
End-time! Showdown-time! Good vs Evil, with
Angels praising, adoring the enthroned Lamb.

They hold sealed scrolls, trumpet weal and woe--
And Archangel Michael combats the Devil-Dragon
In defense of the Woman and her Child. But ah!
The Child has grown. He and the heavenly host
Are clothed in white and mounted on white steeds.
In heaven? Militancy, Whiteness? Words, words--
Sans matter from the heart. Seer John may

Or may not be Evangelist John. No problem--
For both of them the living heart of God's Word
Is love. God is Love; Love is Light, and--God
Be praised--the kaleidoscopic spectrum
Of Love-Light is all colors! Come, Jesus,
Come! Sweep us all up and away with You.

Pentimento

From *pentirsi, to repent,* denoting paintings
Done over by the artist--like Jan Van Eyck's
"The Arnolfini Portrait." Infra-red photos show
The master altered the groom's right hand
In the original. So be it. But why "repentance"?
For what? More to the point: creative change!

An inner dynamic, grounded in the artist's
Signature synergy of brain, heart, and gut,
Impels him or her to strive and keep on
Striving to give form to an inspiration--
Be it only modification of a hand gesture
Distinctive of a pensive Flemish burgher

At his wedding. Art rooted in life! Change,
Creative transformation, revealing the quest
Of a vision! Luminously personified in
The Son of God, iconic Logos, Artist
Supreme, in and through whom, and unto
Whom all creatures are created; who, first,

In Mary's womb, then on Mount Calvary,
Definitively in the garden tomb, enfleshed
The greatest of pentimenti.

Dancing the Glory Be

"What then shall we say to this?"
--Romans 8: 31

Now, at this moment, within the Trinity,
Beats a human heart, the heart of Jesus
Risen; it beats with unconditional love
For us. Glorious mystery!

Heavenly eternity! How can we thrill
To its beat already here on planet Earth?
Words fall short; but good works, deeds done
With love, hit the right note.

Even the simplest little everyday deeds
Count--those corporal and spiritual works
Of mercy by which we enter one another's
Messy worlds and serve there.

On a lighter note or (*pace* Milton)
"Tripping as we go on the light fantastic
Toe," we in our own joyful way rejoice
With King David, dancing

With abandon before the ark of the Covenant;
With Gene Kelly, exuberantly dancing in
The rain; with debonair Fred Astair, dancing
Off the wall, in mid-air. Glory be!

Perichoresis

Abba
Sophia
Ruah
    eternally
      ecstatically
    dancing

and from
their dancing
arise the sun

    and the moon
all of creation
whirling joyfully

round Triune One
    God Father Son
      And Spirit Holy

Mirroring Fragments

Kaleidoscopes! Uncle Joe--God bless him--
Bachelor, always good and kind to us kids,
Gifted me with one skillfully handmade by him,
Giving me my first in-sights into how beautiful
Fragments, even the littlest bits, can be.

Bits of wood, metal, glass in various colors,
Intermingling with grains of silver, gold, all
In mirroring light; now shake the scope even
Ever so gently, and voila! Beauty ever new.
And since bits of matter are playing their parts,

Sophia in her infinite wisdom alone knows
How ancient the new display--wonder
Of wonders--may well be. Relevant question:
Will the cosmic kaleidoscope ever be still;
Will beauty, once and for all eternal, be

Unchanging in form? Ah, "kaleidoscope"--
Metaphor, with its human all too human limits.
For what is deep-down the matter at stake?
Love--the infinite love of God Triune, ever so
Lovingly, lastingly, shepherding ongoing creation;

We, integral parts within the redeemed whole--
Distinguished by our likeness to God's Son
Sempiternally enfleshed--with grateful love
In our hearts, eternally . . infinitely . .
Asymptotically . . approaching . .
God, Beauty, All in all . . .

Grammar of the Word

Singularly substantive
Divinely co-creative
The Word beyond common
And even proper noun

Beyond conception
Beyond declension
Uniquely Love-Verb
Present with creative verve

In epiphany on epiphany
Conjugated in-finitely
In tense and mood
Then in time's plenitude

Time refreshed
Word enfleshed
With new-found voice of action
Sounding the depths of passion

Re-creative ways of being
And doing and being
Done in   on the way to new birth
New heavens   new earth

Beyond judgment and sentence
Enchanting verse on verse
Chanting God All-in-all harmonious
Euphonious   luminous   glorious

Uni-Verse beyond declension
Beyond conception

123

G—D

Three-personed One
   Called and called upon
      By name after name

Beyond all naming
   Numinous No-thing
      Without and within

The Uni-verse
   Fathering us
      Mothering us

Calling us all to be
  From 0-ness One with Mystery
    For ever and ever.   Glory be!